Nuffield Design and Technology

Textiles
Resource Books

Textiles resource tasks

Editor: David Barlex

Contributors: David Barlex, Eileen Barlex, Elizabeth Knief, Ruth Wright, Julie Messenger

Illustrations: Nathan Barlex

We arc grateful to Colin Whitfield for his advice on safety matters. Every effort has been taken to ensure safe practice.

Addison Wesley Longman Limited

Edinburgh Gate, Harlow, Essex, CM20 2JE

© The Nuffield Foundation 1996

First published in 1996
ISBN 0582 29077 5
Set in Times 10/13
Printed by Pindar plc
Design by Stephen I Pargeter, Banbury

The Publishers policy is to use paper manufactured from sustainable forests.

Contents

Textile Resource Tasks

Lines of interest

Health and safety

Products and applications

Part 1

1   Think about the people in the illustration. They are visiting the textiles and haberdashery stall in their local market.

2   Discuss with a partner the different needs and likes of these people. You should both record what you decide in your own workbooks.

Think and talk about these people by using the PIES approach. List the likely physical, intellectual, emotional and social needs of each person or group of people.

 Learning

To identify needs and likes.

 Student's Book

Identifying needs and likes, pages 74–77

 Timing

Part 1: 40 minutes
Part 2: 40 minutes

 Equipment and materials

- workbook
- pen, pencil
- scissors
- glue
- A3 stiff paper card
- magazines
- catalogues
- film and video fliers

 Type of task

Recap

3   Consider what sort of questions you might ask these people if you had the chance to interview them. Note these down for each person or group of people.

Further/homework

Using magazines, supplier catalogues, and samples of cloth and haberdashery, collect information and images that may help to explain the needs and likes of one person or one group of people shown in the illustration.

Part 2

1   Choose one person or one group of people shown in the illustration in Part 1.

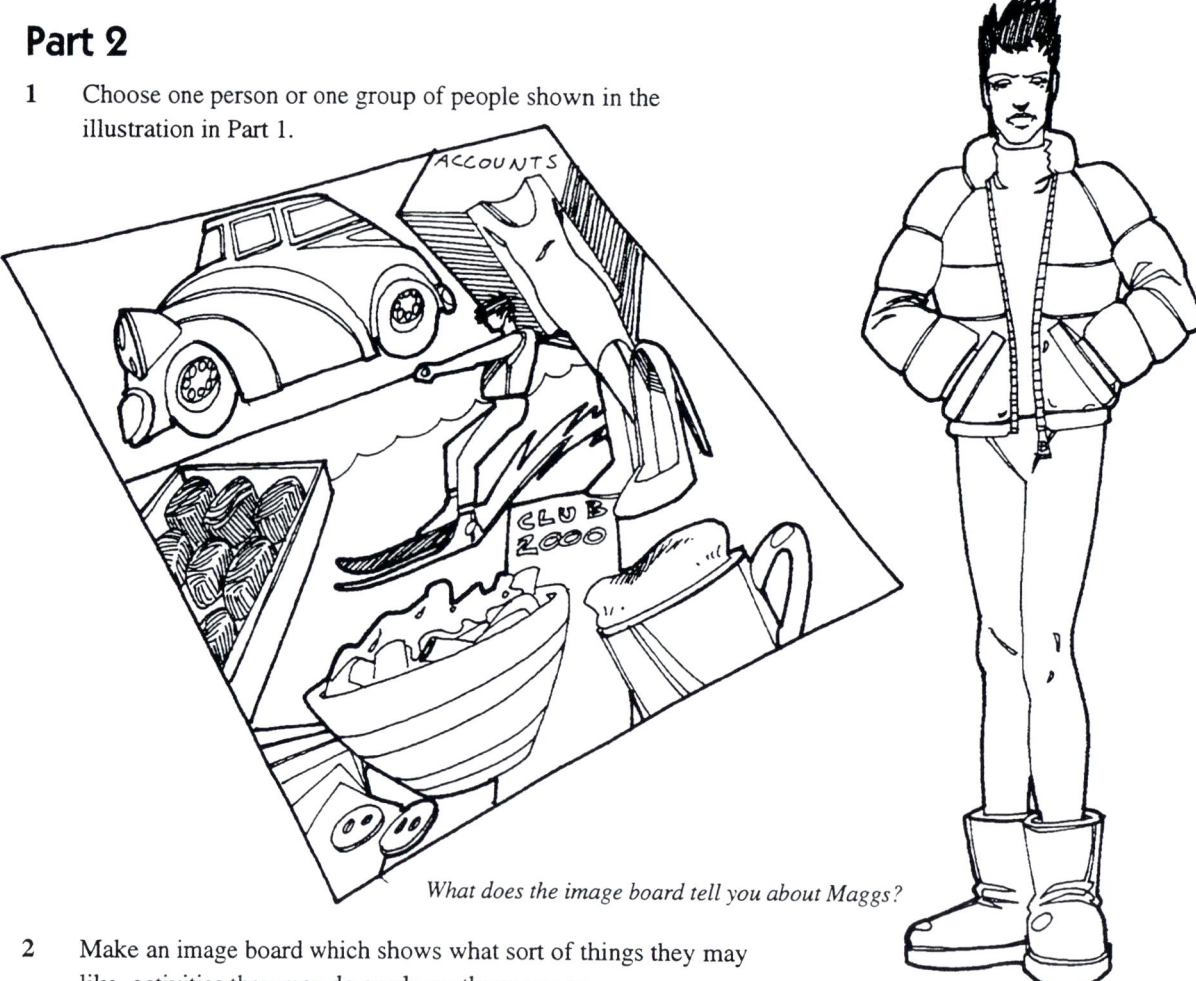

What does the image board tell you about Maggs?

2   Make an image board which shows what sort of things they may like, activities they may do or places they may go.

3   Add to your board some market-related products that they may like. Emphasise the style of these products.

4   Discuss your finished board with a partner.

- Do you agree or disagree that it fits with the character or characters chosen and the market situation?
- Is there anything you have missed or might have thought about more carefully?

What is a database?

A database is a collection of information. A database on a computer makes the information easy to find and use. Many libraries now have their book catalogues on a database.

Imagine that 20 people in your class all collect five sets of data. This is 100 records. Looking through this information would take quite a long time. Looking through a library catalogue would take much longer. Using a database saves time. It also allows you to set up ways of searching the records.

Terms related to a database

A **record** is the information collected about one person or item.

A **field** is a heading in a record.

Here is some information about a textile product in a magazine:

All the information in the box is a record.

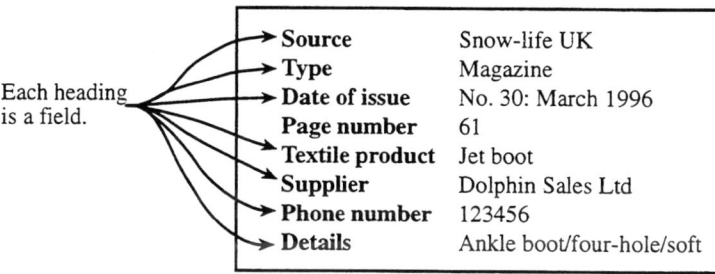

Source	Snow-life UK
Type	Magazine
Date of issue	No. 30: March 1996
Page number	61
Textile product	Jet boot
Supplier	Dolphin Sales Ltd
Phone number	123456
Details	Ankle boot/four-hole/soft

Each heading is a field.

Part 1 The old-fashioned way!

1   Use the questionnaire sheet and fill it in for five families.

2   In class, work with four other people. Put all your questionnaire sheets in a pile. Choose one person to look for information, the others will ask the questions. In your group, work out some questions to ask and write these down. Here are some examples to get you started:

'How many adults in the sample?'
'How many children under 10 years?'
'How many males over 18 years sew on a button at least once a month?'

L Learning

- To use information collected in a survey.
- To use a database to handle the information.

Student's Book

Questionnaires, pages 76–77

Timing

120 minutes

Equipment and materials

- workbook
- pen, pencil
- the questionnaire sheet
- a tally sheet
- access to a computer workstation, with database software

t Type of task

New

Other subjects

IT

3 Ask the person who is responsible for looking for information the questions. Record the answers on a tally sheet like the one in the illustration. Time how long it takes for them to work out the answers.

4 Work out how long it would take for one person to look through the questionnaire sheets for the whole class.

Part 2 The IT way

1 Using a word-processing software package, write out the questions which you thought up in Part 1. When everyone in the group has written out their questions, use a 'cut and paste' facility to produce a whole class composite list of questions.

2 Enter the information from your five questionnaire sheets into a database. Make sure that you save your data! Everyone else in the class will put their information into the database so there will be data from about 100 questionnaires when everyone is finished.

3 Use the list of questions which you prepared in Part 1. Make a search of your database to provide the answers. Record the answers on your question sheet. Time how long it takes to research the answers.

4 Use information presentation software to produce a visual representation of the information you have discovered in the database.

Further/homework

1 Devise a questionnaire which will gather information about one of the following items with a view to identifying ideas for new products:

- soft furnishings;
- wearing of hats/headgear;
- toiletry bags;
- carrying things;
- cuddly toys.

2 Enter the results in a database and interrogate the database to obtain useful information.

Interviewers name _____

Sewing habits in a household

Use a fresh sheet for each new household.

1　How many people are there in the household?

2　How many adults? (18 years plus)
　　Number of males?

　　Number of females?

3　How many children aged 0–10 years?
　　Number of boys?

　　Number of girls?

4　How many teenagers aged 11–17 years?
　　Number of boys?

　　Number of girls?

5　How many working sewing machines do you have in your house?

6　How many not-working sewing machines do you have in your house?

7　Are there any of the following hand-sewing items in your house?

　　a　Cutting-out shears

　　b　Small, sharp pointed scissors

　　c　Sewing needles

　　d　Spools of black and white thread

　　e　Pins

8　How often does each person:

　　a　sew on a button by hand?
　　b　use a sewing machine to mend something?
　　c　use a sewing machine to make something new?
　　d　mend something (other than buttons) by hand-stitching?
　　e　make something new by hand-stitching?

Record the answers on the grid on page 4.

Questionnaire sheet

Name of person	Name of person	Name of person
Male/Female Age Under 11/11–17/18+	Male/Female Age Under 11/11–17/18+	Male/Female Age Under 11/11–17/18+
a Sew on button by hand Never/rarely/once a year/ a few times a year/ every month/ once a week/more often	**a** Sew on button by hand Never/rarely/once a year/ a few times a year/ every month/ once a week/more often	**a** Sew on button by hand Never/rarely/once a year/ a few times a year/ every month/ once a week/more often
b Use machine to mend Never/rarely/once a year/ a few times a year/ every month/ once a week/more often	**b** Use machine to mend Never/rarely/once a year/ a few times a year/ every month/ once a week/more often	**b** Use machine to mend Never/rarely/once a year/ a few times a year/ every month/ once a week/more often
c Use machine to make something new Never/rarely/once a year/ a few times a year/ every month/ once a week/more often	**c** Use machine to make something new Never/rarely/once a year/ a few times a year/ every month/ once a week/more often	**c** Use machine to make something new Never/rarely/once a year/ a few times a year/ every month/ once a week/more often
d Mend by hand Never/rarely/once a year/ a few times a year/ every month/ once a week/more often	**d** Mend by hand Never/rarely/once a year/ a few times a year/ every month/ once a week/more often	**d** Mend by hand Never/rarely/once a year/ a few times a year/ every month/ once a week/more often
e Hand-stitch something new Never/rarely/once a year/ a few times a year/ every month/ once a week/more often	**e** Hand-stitch something new Never/rarely/once a year/ a few times a year/ every month/ once a week/more often	**e** Hand-stitch something new Never/rarely/once a year/ a few times a year/ every month/ once a week/more often

Part 1 Design briefs

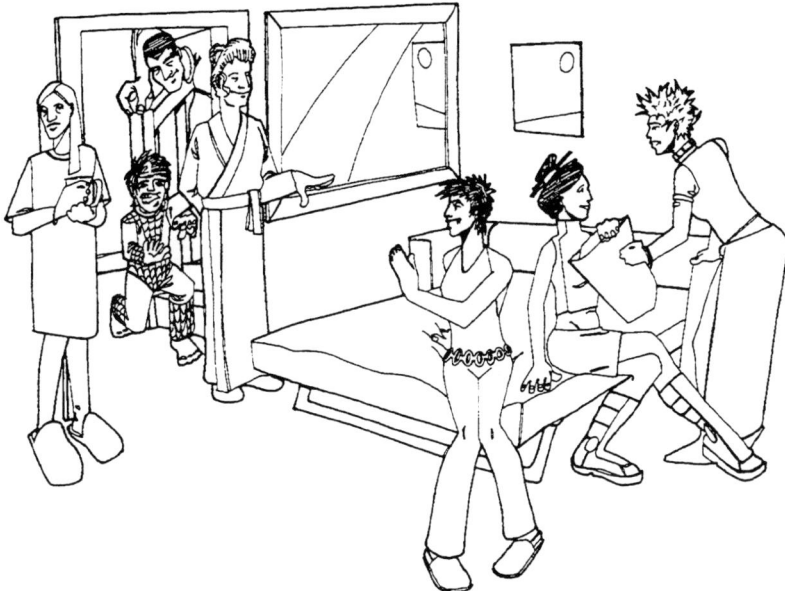

Why do friends come to stop over just when everyone else is at home?

L Learning

- To write design briefs in response to needs, wants and likes.
- To write a specification from a design brief.

Student's Book

Design briefs and Specifying the product, pages 78–80

Timing

Part 1: 40 minutes
Part 2: 40 minutes

Equipment and materials

- workbook
- pen, pencil

t Type of task

Extension

Why does back-garden basketball have to stop when evening comes?

How can the baby, the chair and the floor stay clean?

How can feet be stylishly protected from very hot sand and prickly sea-life?

Each illustration shows a problem situation.

Each caption highlights possible needs, wants or likes.

1   With a partner or in a group of three, talk about each situation
     shown. Discuss some of the possible needs, wants and likes of
     each situation.

2   For each situation, agree (a) a closed brief and (b) an open brief.

3   For each situation, write in your workbook the agreed closed
     brief and open brief.

Further/homework

1   Choose one of the open briefs you have agreed.

2   Break this down into as many closed briefs as you can.

3   Write these down.

Part 2 Specifications

Brief 1 *Design and make a plaited and coiled straw Easter bonnet for a 4-year-old*

plaited, coiled straw

silk fabric flowers

over-sized look

Brief 2 *Design and make a fabric roll for storing and carrying spanners*

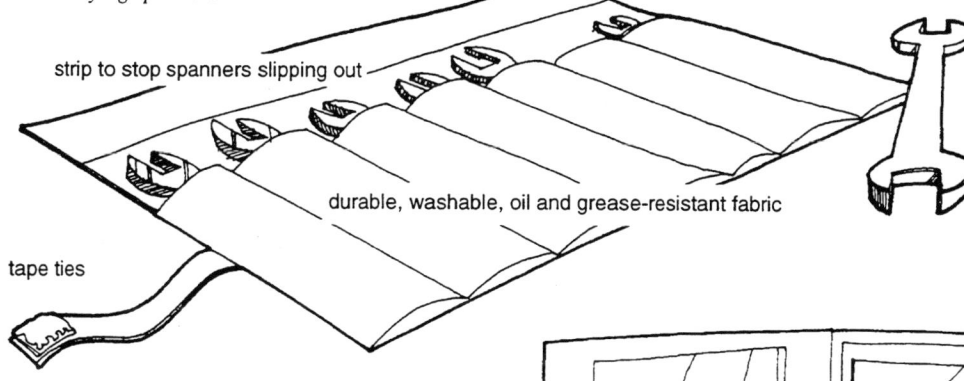

strip to stop spanners slipping out

durable, washable, oil and grease-resistant fabric

tape ties

Brief 3 *Design and make an affordable shelter for homeless people*

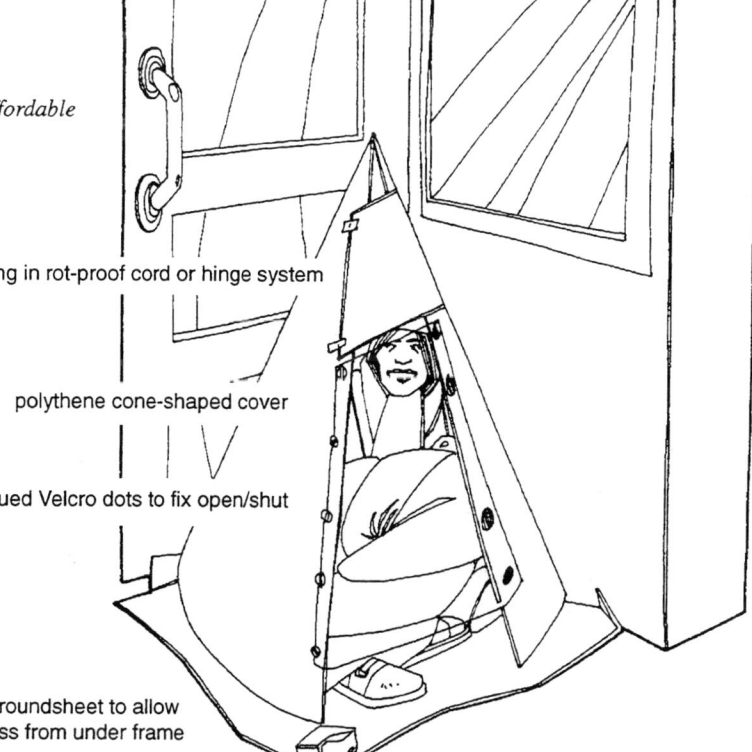

lashing in rot-proof cord or hinge system

polythene cone-shaped cover

door cover with glued Velcro dots to fix open/shut

separate groundsheet to allow quick access from under frame

Brief 4 *Design and make a prototype of an inexpensive costume for a dance piece 'Aftermath of War'*

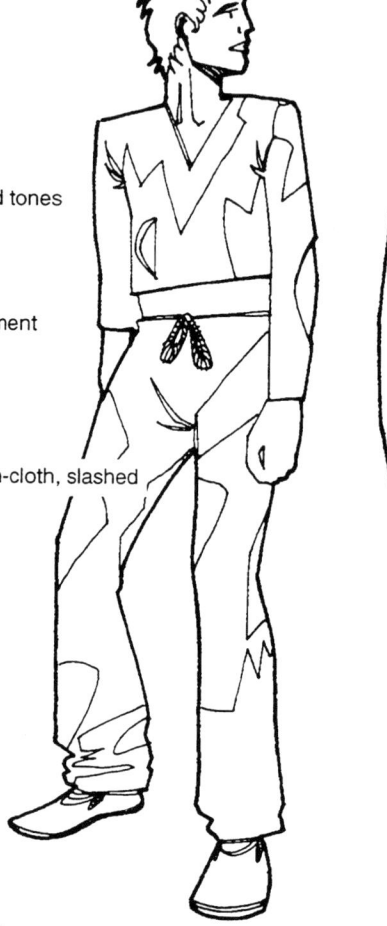
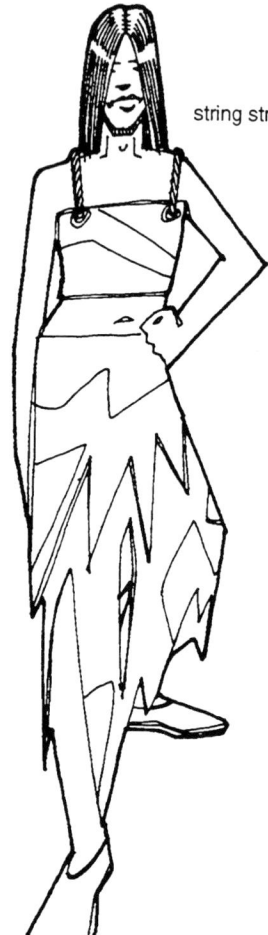

string straps

repeat dip-dyed to get graded tones

lots of room for movement

tubular dish-cloth, slashed

Each illustration shows a product designed to meet the need stated in the brief.

1   Think about each product and design brief carefully.

2   Write a performance specification for each one in your workbook. Use sketches where these help explain your points.

3   Your specification should:

   • describe what the product has to do;
   • describe what the product should look like;
   • state any other requirements that need to be met – how the product should work, manufacturing methods, materials, ergonomic/environmental/legal requirements, etc.

4   Sketch a further product to meet the need in one of the design briefs.

5   Write a performance specification for your solution.

Further/homework

Using your sketch and performance specification from Part 2, for each one develop more detailed sketch drawings of parts of your product. Add notes to show how these details might help meet the specification points.

Brainstorming

Part 1 What can I use for this?

The illustrations below show two design and make situations.

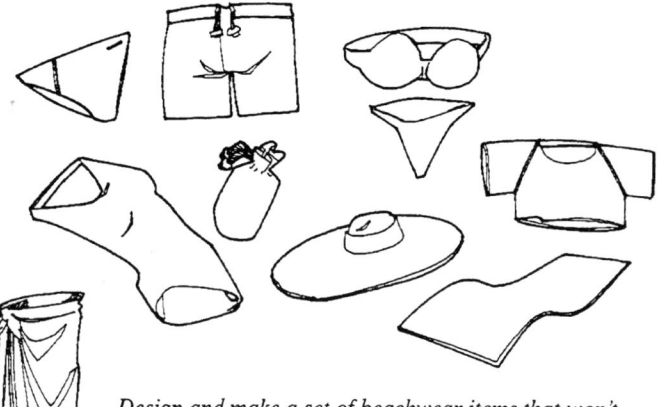

Design and make a set of beachwear items that won't crush and that pack into a small space

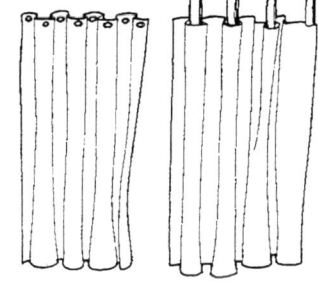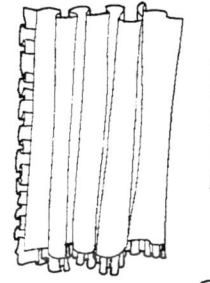
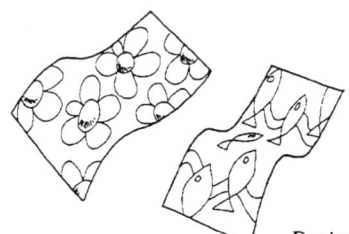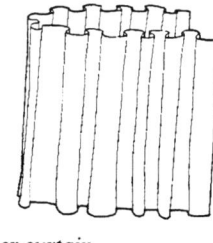

Design and make a shower curtain

 Learning

To apply two sorts of brainstorming.

 Student's Book

Brainstorming, page 81
PIES, page 82
Chooser Charts,
pages 99–100

 Timing

Part 1: 40 minutes
Part 2: 40 minutes

 Equipment and materials

- large sheets of paper
- fat pens
- coloured pens
- work-book
- pen, pencil

 Type of task

Extension

1. In a group of at least three, brainstorm each situation using words, phrases or sketches. Put down every idea you think of. Use who? what? why? when? and where? questions to help you.

   Use the Chooser Charts and PIES heading to help you answer the questions.

2. In your group, agree and circle in different colours which ideas are:

   - most unusual;
   - most interesting;
   - easier to make but also unusual or interesting;
   - harder to make but also unusual or interesting.

3   Agree which ideas are both interesting and could, realistically, be made by you.

4   List these agreed possible ideas for each situation in your workbook.

5   Try to put the ideas into categories – groups of ideas that seem to go together.

6   Make a priority list for each situation – the most important ideas (or groups of ideas) first, and so on.

Further/homework

1   Choose one of the situations from page 1.

2   Using your priority list of ideas for that situation, sketch a product that you could make which would provide a possible solution.

3   Write a performance specification for your product.

Part 2 What can I use this for?

The illustration below shows four different items:

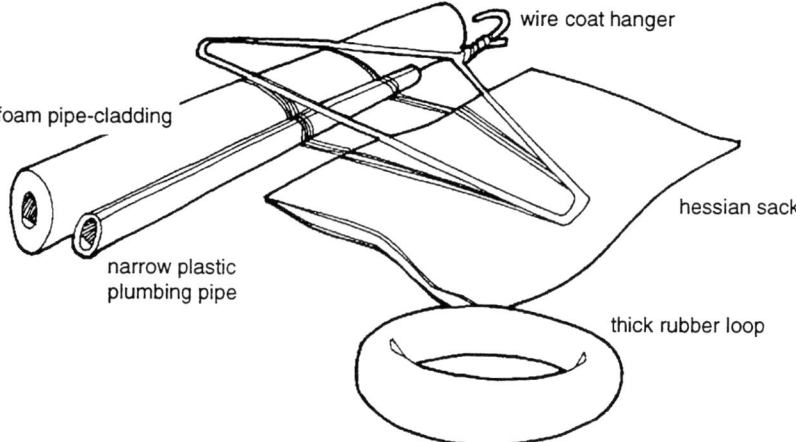

wire coat hanger

foam pipe-cladding

hessian sack

narrow plastic plumbing pipe

thick rubber loop

1   In a group of at least three, brainstorm each item. Using words, phrases or sketches, generate a list of possible uses for each item in the design of a baby carrier that leaves both hands free and in the design of costumes for a school play about a giant and some dwarfs. Put down everything you think of.

2   In your group, agree and circle in different colours which possibilities are:

  • most unusual;
  • most interesting;
  • easier to make but also unusual or interesting;
  • harder to make but also unusual or interesting.

3   Agree which possible uses are both interesting and could, realistically, be made by you.

4   In your workbook list these agreed possible ideas for each design.

The attribute analysis table below describes different aspects of toiletry carriers. The first line of the table describes the attributes of the draw-string soap-bag shown in the illustration.

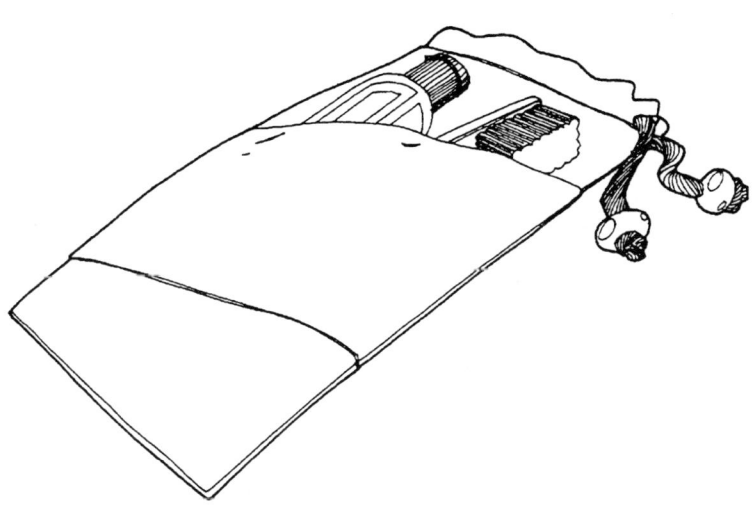

L **Learning**

To extend your understanding of how to use attribute analysis to think up different ideas for a product.

Student's Book

Attribute analysis, page 83

Timing

45 minutes

Equipment and materials

• workbook
• pen, pencil

t **Type of task**

Extension

1   Look across the columns in the attribute analysis table. Select words from each column, putting them together in different combinations to give you new ideas for toiletry carriers. List as many different combinations as you can in the time available to you. (There are almost 20,000 possible variations!)

Material	Properties	Image	Cost	Weight	Manufacture
Day-glo Ripstop Nylon	Waterproof	Street style	Inexpensive	Very light	Mass
Towelling	Strong	Hi-tech	Moderate	Light	One-off
PVC	Resilient	Feminine	Expensive	Medium	Batch
Calico	Rotproof	Masculine		Heavy	
Mesh	Inflammable	Children's			
Metallic	Crush-proof	Green			
Polyester	Washable	Outdoor			
Aluminium	Disposable	Smart			
Plastic	Colour-fast	Casual			
Rubber	Stores things safely				
Non-woven	Hangs up				

Attribute analysis table for toiletry carriers

2   Look at the different combinations on your list. Some of the
    ideas may seem impossible to achieve. If you are not
    sure:

*   discuss with a partner;
*   using the PIES approach for each idea, find out
    what physical, intellectual, emotional and social
    needs it meets that the original idea did not;
*   ask yourself 'Who might this idea
    appeal to that the original did not?'

3   List those product ideas which you think
    could actually be made.

One team lay the cloth

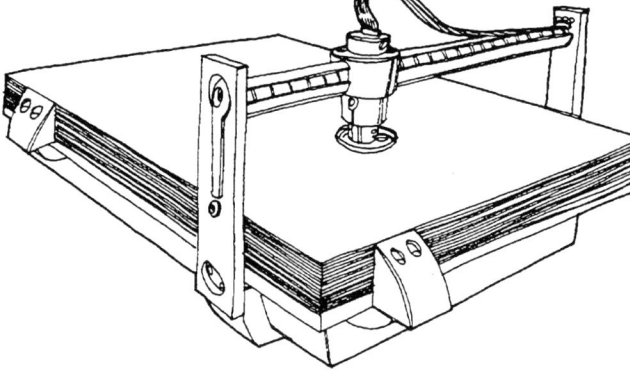

The cords are cut to length

The cloth is cut using a computerized laser cutter

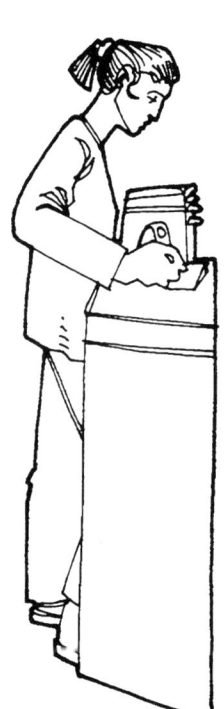

*The machining team stitch the elastic into the pocket hem, they stitch on the
pocket and stitch the sides of the bag and make the top channels – with the
cords in place. (In some companies some of this stitching is automated)*

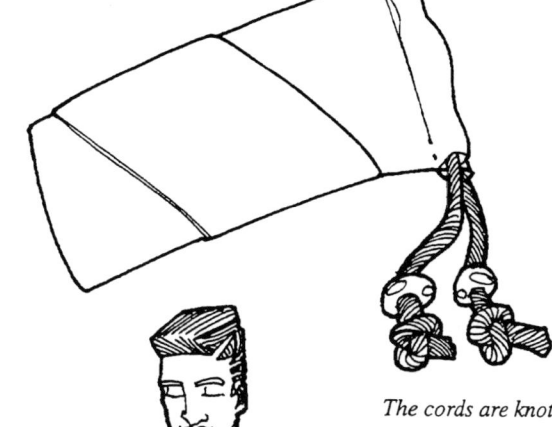

The cords are knotted

4 Consider the manufacturing methods already used to produce the draw-string soap-bag shown on page 1.

This soap-bag is mass manufactured. The workers work in teams as shown below.

A further team makes final quality checks and packs the soap-bags

At each stage in manufacturing the soap-bag the team responsible for the work is responsible for ensuring quality

5 Choose one or two of the product ideas that you listed in number **3**. For each idea work out what you would need in terms of:

- materials;
- equipment;
- quality checks and controls.
- processes;
- skills of workers;

6 Which of your ideas would be suitable for development by the company making the product shown in the illustration?

Further/homework

1 Draw up an attribute analysis table for a family tent.

2 What headings will you need?

3 Fill in some different attributes in each column.

4 Sketch one example of a different family tent suggested by your table.

Part 1

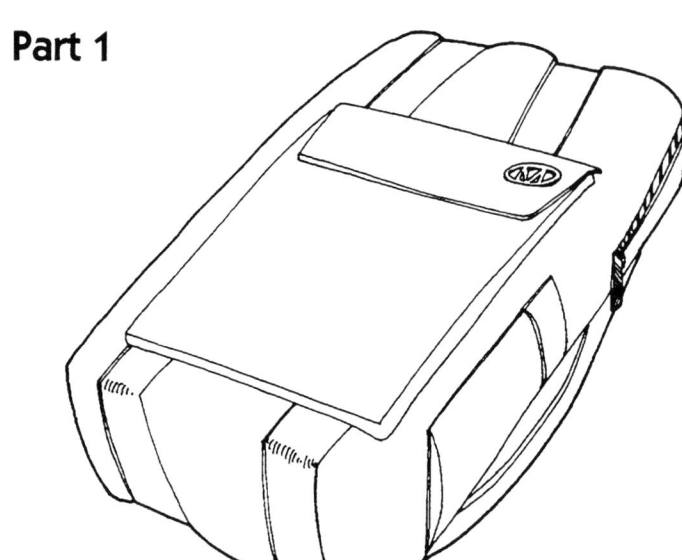

The backpack shown in the illustration has been designed as a promotional gift for the staff, models and clients of a model agency. The backpack includes the agency logo and is shaped to hold an A4 portfolio.

Learning

To extend your understanding of how to evaluate a design by thinking how it affects people, whether it performs as expected and whether it is appropriate.

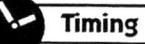

Student's Book

Evaluating, pages 96–98

Timing

Part 1: 40 minutes
Part 2: 40 minutes

Equipment and materials

- workbook
- pen, pencil
- highlighters

Type of task

Extension

1   Think about who the recipients and users might be.

2   Using the User Trip approach, note down some questions you might ask people about this product.

3 Make two lists – one for the likely recipients and one for the likely users.

The performance specification for this product might look like this:

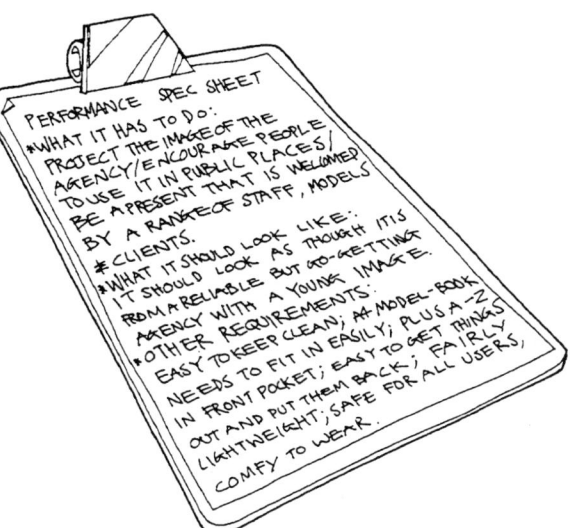

4 Think about what questions you might ask which would help you to compare the performance of this product against the specification.

Will they all like this? Who else might use it? What do they need to fit into it? Will it protect the contents? Is it comfy to wear? Easy to carry? Does it project the right image?

5 Write a list of these questions in your workbook.

6 Are any of the User Trip questions and the Performance Testing questions similar?

7 Highlight any similar questions in the same colours.

Further/homework

1 Draw up a simple chart of User Trip questions and/or Performance Testing questions for a textile product that you have at home – for example a sleeping-bag, a tea-cosy, bath-robe.

2 Identify four or five likely users of the product.

3 Ask the users the questions. Record their answers in writing or on audiotape.

Part 2

So, where do these grow?
Who harvests them? What energy sources
are needed for synthetic and natural dyeing? How much
energy? What about transporting raw materials,
dyes, dyed cloth or made items on an
international scale?

If natural dyes were to be used on a wide scale there might be certain problems.

Synthetic fibres were not around before synthetic dyes were introduced. Natural dyes have an affinity with natural fibres and are not generally suitable for dyeing synthetic fibres.

Mordants (such as tin, lead, chrome, copper, alum and iron) are often used in the natural dyeing processes to increase the fastness of the dyes. They also allow a wider range of hues to be obtained from the same natural substance. However, if these mordants are discharged into effluent they can cause toxic pollution; legislation currently restricts their use because of this.

Natural dyes require quite large quantities of natural resources to produce even small amounts of dye. For example:

* 155,000 dried cochineal insects are needed to produce 1 kilogram of red cochineal dye;
* 140 crocus stigmas supply 1 gram of dyestuff;
* 12,000 Purpura or Murex shellfish are required for 1.4 grams of Tyrian purple (which is why only Roman nobles wore this rare purple colour).

Natural dyes have always been associated with difficulties in colour-fastness (they are 'fugitive'). For example, they may fade quickly in sunlight.

On the other side of the picture is the consideration that the chemical industry is powerful and international.

In many developing countries natural dyestuffs are used to produce fibres and goods – some which reflect their own culture – for more wealthy markets. They can often produce goods more cheaply and currently consumers are showing preferences for many products which seem to be more 'natural'.

Establishing chemical-based dyeing plants in such countries might reduce environmental hazards from mordant toxic waste but might also have long-term impact on the culture and degree of independence from outside control. Local workers would need to be trained in new skills and, possibly, dyeing with synthetics would be less labour-intensive.

Some people feel that positive action is the best way forward – that research should be encouraged which will explore natural dyeing processes and develop ways of making them safer and better.

1   Use the questions on page 98 of the Student's book: Strategies to think about whether or not a wider-scale use of synthetic dyes is an appropriate thing to encourage.

2   With a partner, discuss answers to these questions and note these in your workbook. Then use another strategy to think about this issue – winners and losers:

   • Draw a winners and losers target chart.
   • Write 'Wider Use of Synthetic Dyes' in the middle.
   • Write down those people directly affected by encouraging a wider use of synthetic dyes in the spaces in the first ring.
   • Write down those indirectly affected by encouraging a wider use of synthetic dyes in the spaces in the outer ring.
   • Highlight the winners in one colour and the losers in another colour.

3   Think about whether this idea is appropriate. Draw up a simple chart like this:

   Column 1: List some questions that you can ask yourself about the idea (your earlier 'is this appropriate' questions may help).

   Column 2: Award marks for each question by using an evaluation scale – for example:

   1 = poor 2 = only adequate 3 = average 4 = good 5 = excellent

   Column 3: Put a reason for why you have awarded each mark.

4   Look at your overall scores and reasons.

5   Compare this chart with your winners and losers target chart from number **2**.

6   Think about:

   • whether this idea seems to be a good or bad one;
   • what the consequences might be;
   • what can be done to make sure that people are not exploited.

7   Write and explain your thoughts in your workbook.

Further/homework

1   Imagine that you are setting up a small-scale business enterprise in your school making batik sarongs using natural dyes.

2   Draw up a winners and losers target chart.

3   Think about whether this idea is appropriate – in your school, your locality, your likely client-market, etc.

4   Note and explain your conclusions.

In this task you will look at the way control is used during the manufacture of fabrics and garments.

1   The list below summarizes the key stages in the production of a shirt made from polyester cotton:

Production of polyester filament
Production of polyester yarn
Production of cotton yarn
Weaving of polyester cotton fabric
Cutting of fabric parts according to pattern
Assembly of fabric parts according to pattern
Addition of fastenings according to pattern
Addition of care labels according to pattern
Folding and packaging

Learning

To apply systems and control concepts to textile product manufacture.

Student's Book

Systems, pages 92–93
Production of yarns, pages 162–163
Weaving, pages 170–171

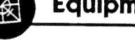

Timing

40 minutes

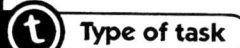

Equipment and materials

• workbook
• pencil

Type of task

Extension

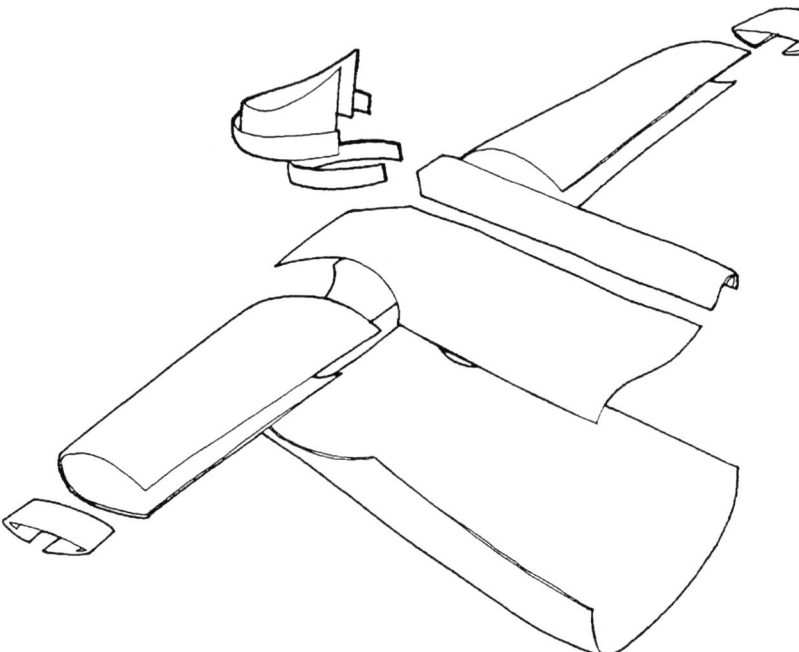

2   Organize these stages into a flow chart.

3   For each of these stages state clearly the following:

  • the machines likely to be used;
  • the role of humans in operating these machines;
  • the role of computers in operating these machines;
  • how the control required to carry out the operations is achieved, including any feedback.

4   At which stage in the production process is majority control by computer replaced by majority control by humans?

Further/homework

Develop a flow chart which summarizes the production of a pair of socks made from polyester cotton. Compare it to the flow chart above. In what ways is it significantly different?

Many textile products are designed with a theme or mood as an important starting point. Mood or theme boards help the designer develop design ideas and also show the client the designer's basic thinking in an extremely visual and easy to understand way. In this task you are required to produce a mood board which communicates one of the following pairs of opposites:

- fiery/cool;
- wet/dry;
- masculine/feminine;
- handmade/mass-produced;
- natural/artificial;
- traditional/modern;
- hi-tech/low-tech.

You cannot show any objects or people, just shapes, colours, patterns and textures. You can cut these from old magazines or scrap fabric. You may be able to use a colour photocopier to create repeat patterns or special effects.

You should assemble your mood board so that it not only communicates the mood but does so in an eye-catching and provocative way. The illustration shows some possibilities. You will find that it helps to work in a group.

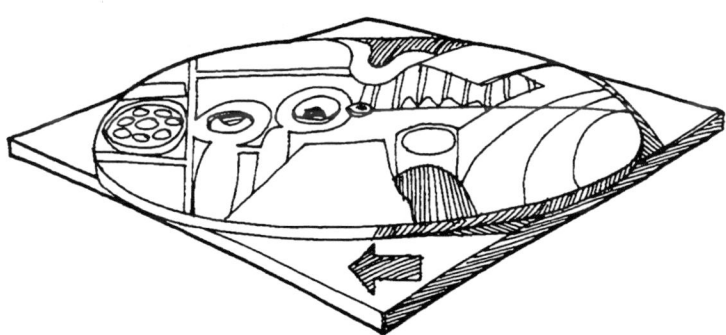

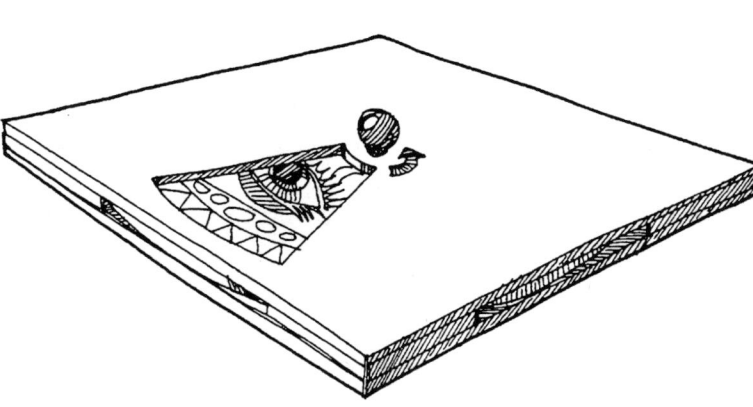

 Learning

To use mood or theme boards to communicate a design idea.

 Student's Book

Communicating design ideas, pages 101–110

 Timing

90 minutes

 Equipment and materials

- A3 or A2 sugar paper
- glue stick or spray mount
- scissors
- craft knife, safety ruler and cutting mat
- access to a wide range of disposable colour magazines
- access to a wide range of scrap fabrics
- access to a colour photocopier if possible

 Type of task

Extension

 Other subjects

Art

SAFETY NOTE

Take extreme care when using the craft knife. Hold the material so that your hand is behind the direction of cutting.

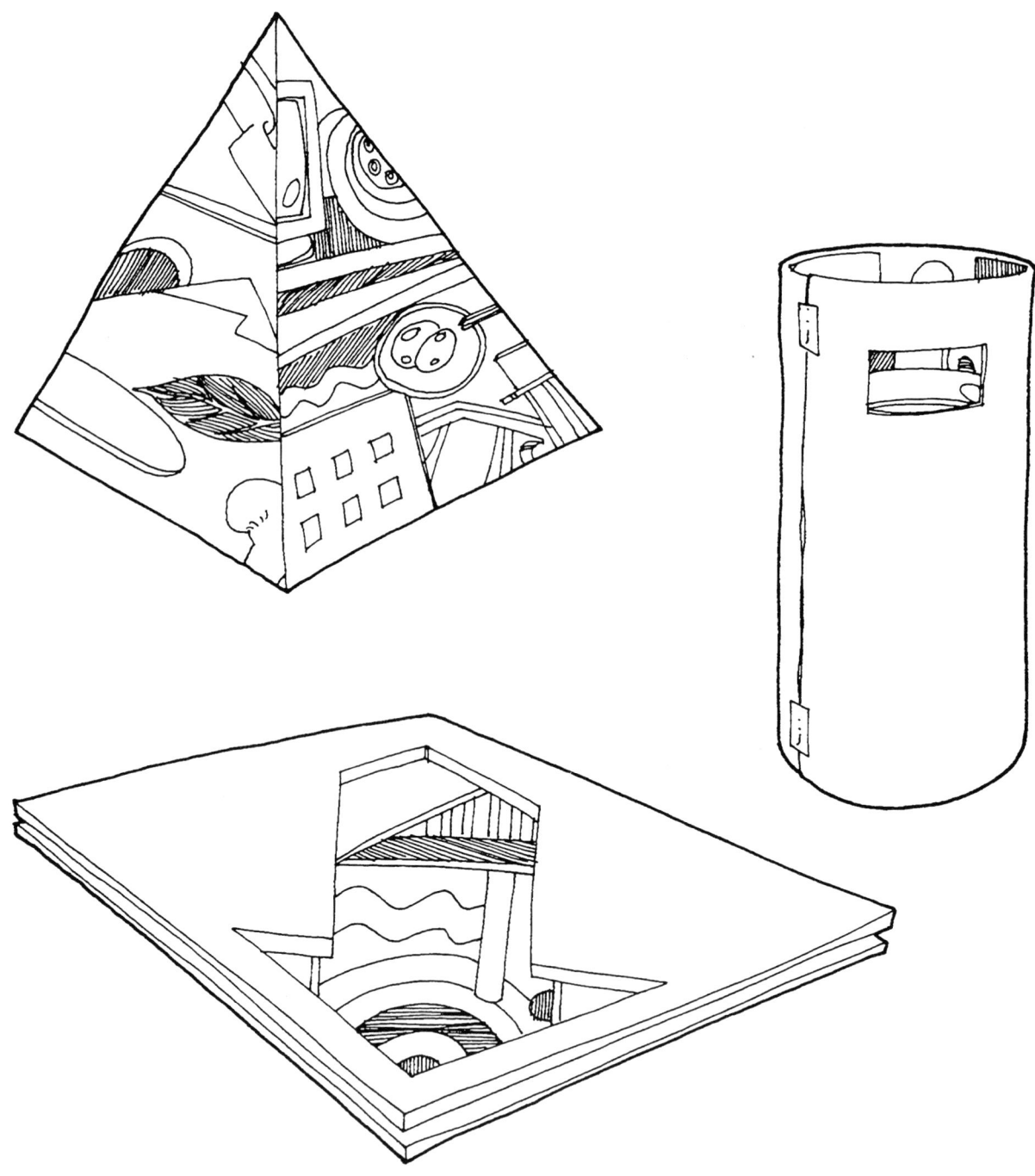

Further/homework

Make a collage of a fashion collection by a currently popular designer and see if you can identify from this the theme or mood that underlies the work.

The table shows some data concerning sales of swimwear through a major retail outlet.

	£ sales per month in 1993	£ sales per month in 1994	£ sales per month in 1995
January	1 k	1 k	2 k
February	2 k	1 k	1 k
March	4 k	3 k	4 k
April	6 k	7 k	3 k
May	10 k	9 k	11 k
June	16 k	17 k	20 k
July	20 k	22 k	20 k
August	25 k	30 k	27 k
September	13 k	10 k	12 k
October	2 k	1 k	2 k
November	1 k	1 k	1 k
December	1 k	0 k	1 k

L Learning

To present data in an easily accessible form.

Student's Book

Communicating your design proposals, pages 101–110

Timing

60 minutes

Equipment and materials

• workbook
• pencil
• graph paper
• ruler
• protractor
• access to computer, printer and graph-drawing software

t Type of task

Extension

Other subjects

IT

1   Use appropriate graphical techniques for the following:

• comparison of sales each month for each year;
• trends in sales during each year;
• proportion of total sales represented by each month's sales for each year.

Draw at least one graph by traditional means – pencil, graph paper, ruler, etc.

Draw at least one graph using IT means.

2   Make sure that both means of presentation are as clear as possible. Check the following:

• titles;
• labelled axes;
• appropriate use of colour;
• appropriate use of supporting illustrations.

Further/homework

Using the data available predict the sales figures for swimwear in 1996 Present you predictions in the form of a graph.

Fashion drawings just create impressions of the clothes and the way they will look. They are usually drawn quickly with felt-tip markers or felt-tip brushes. It takes practice to achieve this.

1 To start with use the outline of a figure in a catwalk pose. Choose one of the poses illustrated here that you like. Then select one of the outfits listed on page 2. Cover the pose you chose with layout paper and quickly mark in the outfit. If it goes wrong just move the layout paper across and have another go. Remember, keep the detail minimal but get the impression right.

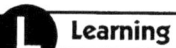 **Learning**

To present ideas for fashion clothes.

 **Student's Book**

Communicating your ideas, pages 101–110

 Timing

90 minutes

 Equipment and materials

• layout paper
• access to marker pens or marker brushes

 Type of task

New

 Other subjects

Art

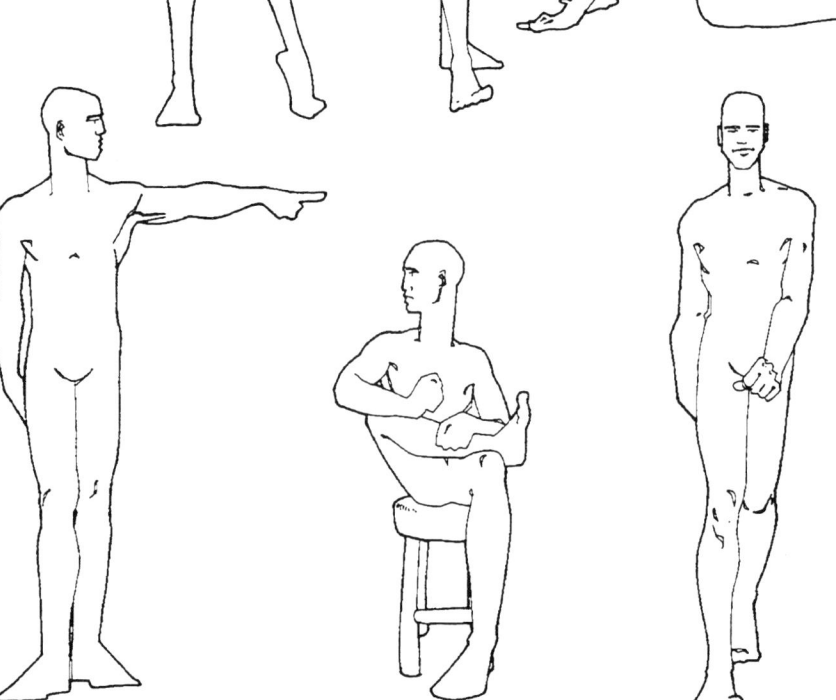

Fashion drawing

Outfit 1

short black skirt
yellow blouse
orange neckerchief
yellow pill-box hat
high-heeled black shoes

Outfit 2

red and white striped dress
chunky red shoes

Outfit 3

blue suit
pink shirt
dark blue suede shoes

Outfit 4

black jeans
red boots
white short-sleeve top
long open sleeveless grey cardigan

Outfit 5

loose-fitting grey jacket
pink shirt
dark tie
dark slacks
black shiny shoes

Outfit 6

long tan shorts
brightly patterned short-sleeve
shirt
no shoes

Outfit 7

blousey loose-fitting top
track suit type bottom trousers
trainers

Outfit 8

well-fitting grey check formal suit
dark blue shirt
pale tie
black shoes

2   Once you feel confident and are getting the effect you want try
to draw some of the outfits without the pose guide.

Further/homework

Develop a series of fashion drawings for an outfit of your choice.

crt 4

Capturing fabric on paper

Here are outline drawings of some fashion accessories with brief notes describing their appearance.

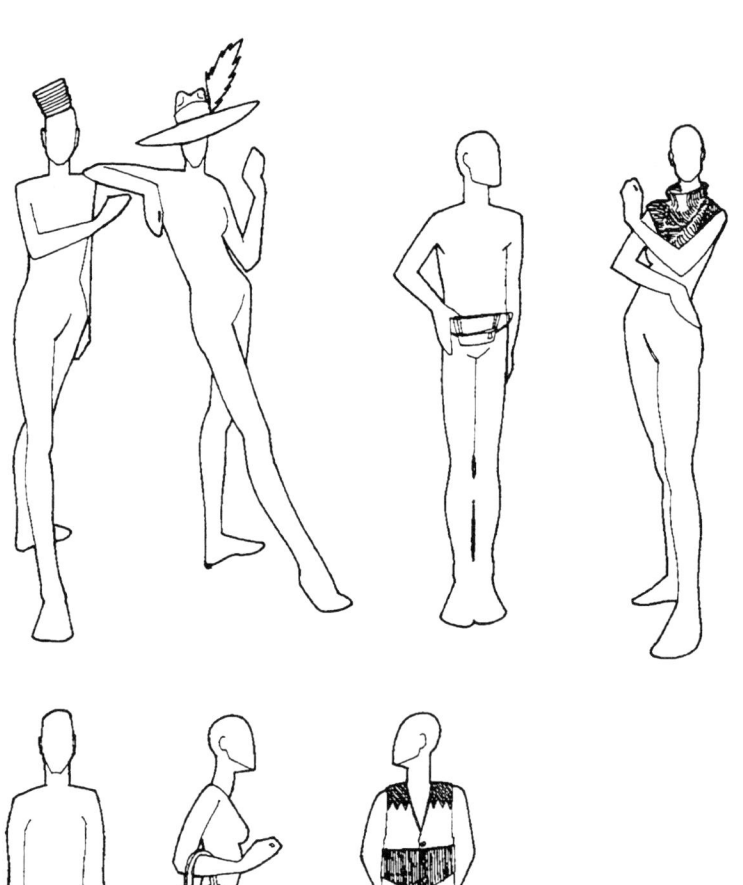

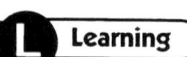

L **Learning**

To draw items made from fabric in a realistic way.

Student's Book

Communicating your ideas, pages 101–110

! **Timing**

90 minutes

Equipment and materials

- cartridge paper
- access to sample materials for swatches

A selection of:
- lead pencils
- coloured pencils
- water-based paints
- felt marker pens

t **Type of task**

New

Other subjects

Art

- pill box hat – brightly stripped, knitted
- floppy felt hat – with hat band and feather decoration
- belt bag – made from brightly coloured canvas with a plastic clip
- scarf made from patterned silk (one side) and woven wool (other side)
- studded leather belt – with shiny metal buckle
- small evening hand bag – made from satin, decorated with sequins and beads
- pannelled waistcoat – made from brown corduroy and blue denim with satin back

1   Choose one or two of these fashion accessories and make a careful pencil drawing of each.

2   Add colour and shading until the appearance of your drawing shows the nature of the fabric(s) from which each item is made.

3   If suitable fabric samples are available, pin example swatches to your drawings.

Further/homework

Choose a garment such as a blouse/shirt or jacket. Make a realistic drawing which shows the item being worn.

Part 1 Through simple colouring

1   The drawing below shows an interior in which there are many textile items: carpets, curtains, rugs, furniture coverings, cushion-covers, wall hangings.

Use an enlarged version of this scene to explore the effect of different textile designs. Here are some options:

(a) plain, muted colours only for all features;
(b) plain colours only but a mixture of bold and muted;
(c) as either (a) or (b) but with the addition of a simple striped pattern;
(d) as either (a) or (b) but with the addition of a floral pattern.

2   Make coloured drawings of at least two different interior designs.

Part 2 Using IT

1   Scan in the interior and use paint software to produce at least four different versions based on the options given in Part 1.

2   Print out your designs.

3   Compare them with those you obtained using coloured pencils and felt-tip markers. Which do you think are the most realistic? Which are the easiest to produce? Which are the easiest to adapt?

Further/homework

Draw a single-point perspective view of your bedroom at home. By simple colouring explore different interior designs.

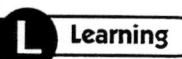

Learning

To show the effect of different textile products on an interior.

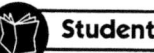

Student's Book

Communicating your design ideas, pages 101–110

Timing

120 minutes

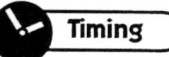

Equipment and materials

Part 1
• coloured pencils
• felt-tip markers

Part 2
• access to computer, paint software and colour printer

(t) Type of task

New

Other subjects

IT

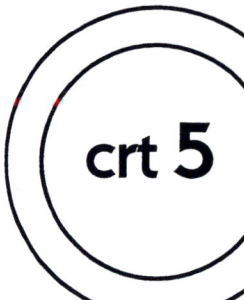
Interior for textile exploration

It is important that all the information required for making is included on a pattern. If this is not the case the person who is to do the making will almost certainly produce a poor-quality item. The diagram below shows the patterns for the pieces needed to make up a blouse. The finished blouse is also shown. However, there are several omissions from the pattern.

L **Learning**

To ensure that information for making textile items is complete.

Student's Book

Communicating your ideas, pages 101–110

Timing

60 minutes

Equipment and materials

- workbook
- pencil

t **Type of task**

New

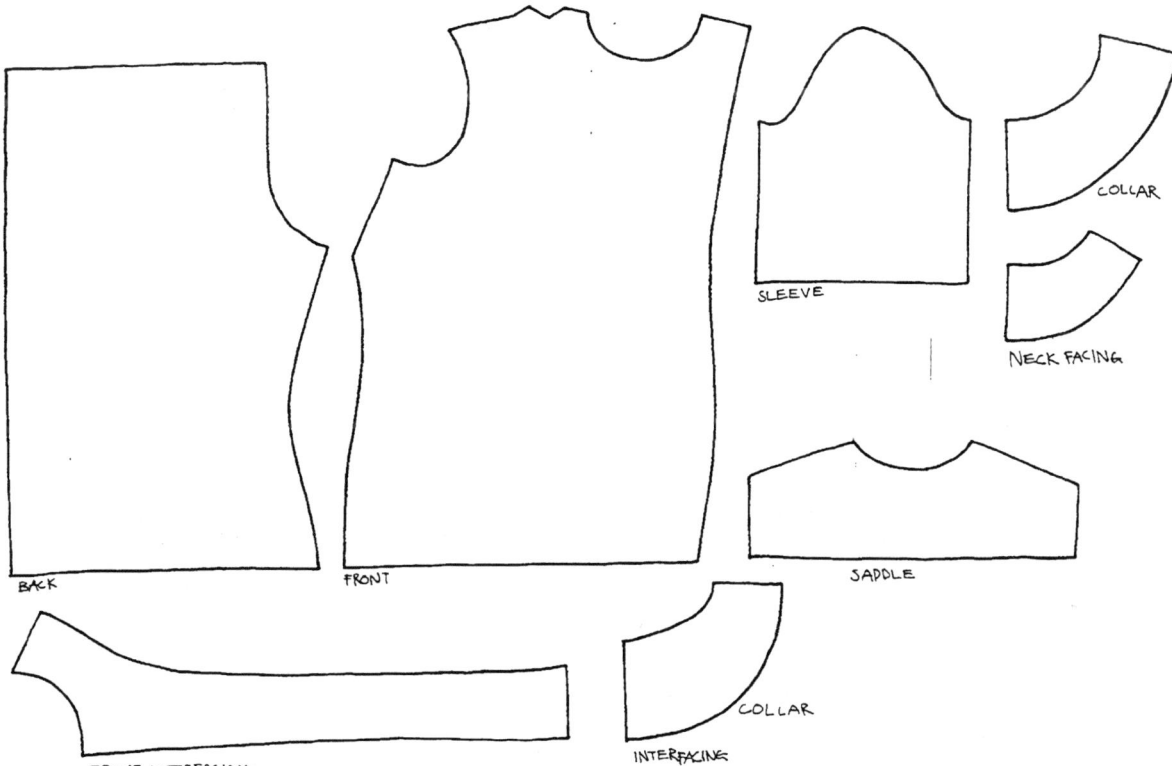

BACK

FRONT

SLEEVE

COLLAR

NECK FACING

SADDLE

FRONT INTERFACING

INTERFACING

COLLAR

Make a neat copy of each pattern piece and mark in the missing information.

mfrt 1

Rally arm bands

Whenever there is a large rally supporting a cause there is the opportunity for textile products – printed T-shirts, head bands, arm bands, banners, fancy dress.

Learning

To design and make a batch of simple textile products.

Student's Book

Systems thinking.
pages 92–93
Street style, pages 121–126

Timing

180 minutes

Equipment and materials

- hand-sewing equipment
- machine-sewing equipment
- block printing equipment

Type of task

New

In this task you will set up a manufacturing system to produce 'rock against racism' arm bands. This will involve the following:

- block printing a logo/symbol onto fabric;
- cutting out badge pieces with the logo/symbol;
- cutting out the fabric pieces for the arm bands;
- attaching the badge to the arm band;
- hemming the arm band;
- attaching Velcro to the arm band.

You will need to work in a group of four. Your teacher will provide you with a printing block for the logo illustrated here, or a similar symbol/logo.

1 Decide which members of the team will carry out which tasks and in what order. Also plan what quality assurance checks can be made to ensure that a consistent product is being made each time.

2 Set up your production system making sure that each member of the team has the necessary tools and equipment.

3 Run the production system and make a batch of 20 arm bands.

4 Randomly select five of the items and evaluate them by using criteria in a table like the one shown here.

	Sample 1	Sample 2	Sample 3	Sample 4	Sample 5
length					
width					
evenness of hem					
evenness of hem stitching					
quality of printing					
evenness of badge stitching					
positioning of badge					
positioning of Velcro					
evenness of Velcro stitching					

5 Comment on the consistency of the feature being examined across the five samples.

6 Explain why five samples were tested rather than just one or two.

7 Comment on your batch production system by answering the following questions.

(a) For how many criteria were all products identical?

(b) For how many criteria were four out of five products identical?

(c) For how many criteria were three out of five products identical?

(d) For how many criteria were two out of five products identical?

(e) For how many criteria were none of the five products identical?

(f) For which criteria did you get at least one satisfactory product?

(g) How could you improve your batch production system to ensure that each product was satisfactory in all the criteria AND identical to every other product produced by the system?

8 Draw a systems diagram to show how materials move through each stage of your improved production and mark in the feedback of information that is required to assure quality products.

Tie-dyeing with natural dyes

You will investigate tie-dyeing wool and unbleached cotton yarns with natural dyestuffs. You can use the dyed yarns for the ikat weaving technique (where a pattern is tie-dyed into the warp threads before weaving) or for knitting a 'random' colour item.

This task will be more useful as an investigation if you work together with three or four others. As a group you can limit the use of mordant, dyestuffs and energy, and have access to a wider range of dyes.

You can use the following materials as natural dyes:

Walnut shells for browns
Onion skins for yellows
Tea (tannin) for oranges/browns
Raspberries for reds/pinks
Lichen for purples
Turmeric for yellows
Beetroot for pinks
Coffee for browns
Flower heads (only use cultivated flowers or garden 'weeds')
All sorts of leaves and bark

 Learning

To carry out tie-dyeing and investigate natural dyes.

 Student's Book

Ways to make your product
– Tie-dyeing, page 150
Technical knowledge –
Dyeing your own yarns,
pages 168–169

 Timing

120 minutes (assuming natural dyestuff available)

 Equipment and materials

• skeins of natural wool yarn and unbleached cotton yarn
• selection of natural materials to make dyestuffs
• access to food processor
• string
• dye-baths and wooden spoons
• heat sources
• alum, cream of tartar
• rubber gloves and aprons
• card, permanent marker
• hole-punch and scissors
• an exercise book
• workbook
• pencil

 Type of task

Recap and Extension

SAFETY NOTE
Remember that any dye stains. Note the following safety points:

• wear rubber gloves and an apron;
• careful use of food blenders if preparing the dye material;
• careful handling of hot dye or mordant solutions;
• careful use of mordants which are toxic or corrosive.

Read through the following instructions carefully. Then in your group work out the most efficient way for you to carry them out.

Frame 1

Getting ready

Use twice the weight of natural raw materials as the weight of yarn you have to dye.

You may need to break or chop up or blend some materials before using them.

Use at least 1 litre of water.

Frame 2

Making the dye

Put raw materials in water in old saucepan or dye-bath. Bring to the boil and simmer. Most materials need to simmer for about an hour to extract all the dye. Roots and barks may take longer.

Frame 3

Preparing the yarn as skeins

Make up skeins of wool and cotton, each of the same weight, by wrapping the yarn round an exercise book five times. Use a tag to label each skein with a number, your name, the dye and the mordant (in this case alum).

Frame 4

Tying the skeins

Tie the skeins so that the dye cannot penetrate evenly. You can use string tied around the skein, knots in the skein and knots in the yarn. Use annotated sketches to record how you have tied each skein.

Frame 5

Wetting the yarn

Add a drop of washing-up liquid to a bowl of water and wet the skeins by immersing in the water for ten minutes.

Frame 6

Preparing the mordant

Use the following recipe for 100 gram yarn:

- 25 g alum;
- 1 tsp cream of tartar;
- 4 litres of water.

Dissolve the alum and cream of tartar in the hot water in a dye-bath. Bring to boil and simmering point.

Frame 7

Using the mordant

Drop the skeins into the mordanting bath and simmer for about one hour. Make sure tags don't get wet or catch fire.

Frame 8

Removing the skeins

Turn off the heat source and remove the skeins from mordanting bath with a wooden spoon or tongs and wet again as in **5**.

Frame 9

Dyeing the yarn

Drop at least one skein into each dyestuff bath. Simmer for about an hour.

Frame 10

Removing the skeins

Turn off the heat source and remove the skeins from the hot dye-baths.

Frame 11

Rinsing

Rinse the skeins gently in warm water.

Frame 12

Untying

Untie all your ties, knots and so forth but leave the label on.

Frame 13

Noting results

Note down the results you have achieved next to your annotated drawings. Also note down the results of others.

Further/homework

Use your results to answer the following questions.

1   How much is the final colour dependent upon:

- the original colour of the yarn?
- the physical condition of the yarn?
- the fibre content of the yarn?
- the dyestuff used?

2   Which results please you most in terms of:

- the colour(s) achieved?
- the pattern(s) achieved?

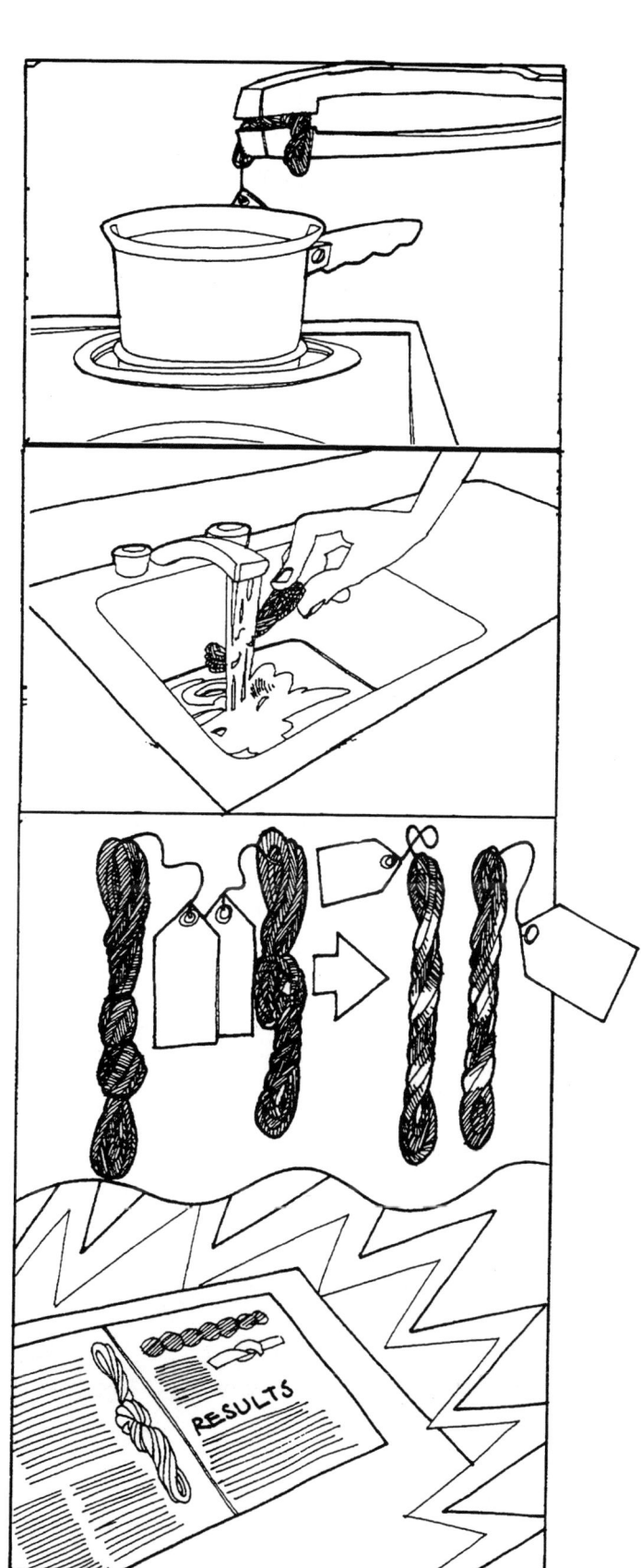

Batik snowflakes

You will produce a sample of hand-decorated fabric using batik. You can use your fabric to make a scarf or head band.

Part 1 Creating the pattern

1   Take two circles of plain paper of exactly the same size and fold the circles together in half, then quarters, then eighths. Try to keep them as flat as possible.

2   When the paper is folded into eighths, use scissors to cut a pattern into the folds of the segment. Try to have some large and some small cut-out areas. Keep your pattern simple. Open out the circles and you should have two identical snowflake patterns.

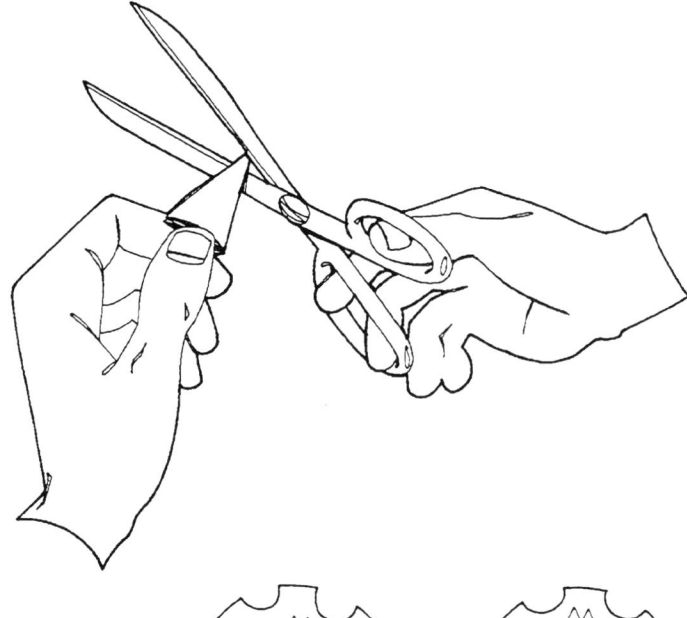

 Learning

To use batik to decorate a small square of fabric that can be made into a scarf or head band.

Student's Book

Ways to make your product: Batik, page 151

 Timing

120 minutes

 Equipment and materials

- access to cold dye of chosen colour
- access to wax heater, double saucepan and melted paraffin wax
- 1 square of washed cotton calico (75 cm x 75 cm)
- tjanting (wax trailer) with narrow spout
- large bristle brush
- 2 sheets of paper (30 cm x 30 cm)
- scissors
- dressmaking pins
- rubber gloves and old newspapers
- iron
- access to sewing machine and thread

 Type of task

New

 Other subjects

Mathematics

3   Cut one circle into quarters, taking care to cut through the centre
of the paper rather than a hole.

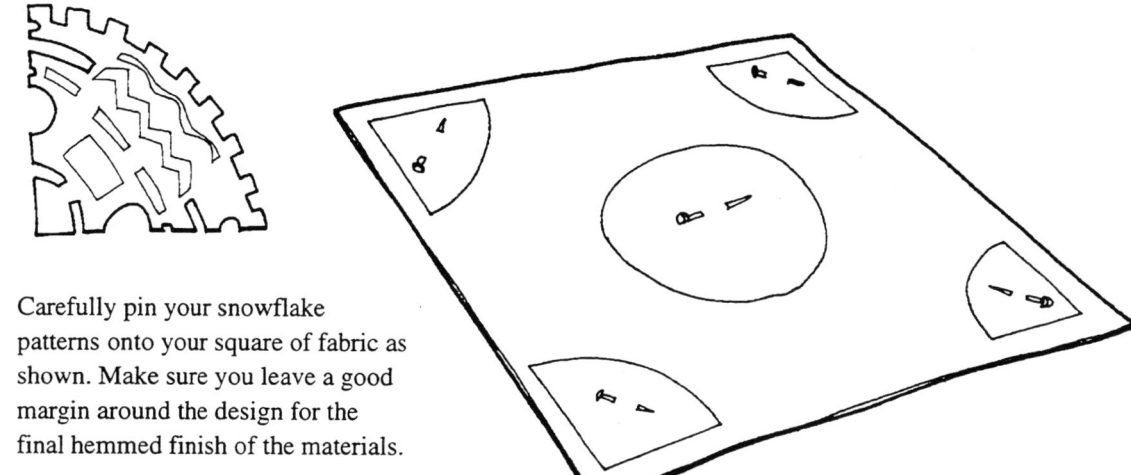

4   Carefully pin your snowflake
patterns onto your square of fabric as
shown. Make sure you leave a good
margin around the design for the
final hemmed finish of the materials.

Part 2 Applying the wax

1   Stretch your prepared fabric over a wad of old
newspapers and apply hot wax to your design
using a paint brush. When all the open areas
in your design have been waxed, additional
linking patterns, using the wax trailer, can be
added.

2   Allow to dry and remove the pins while the wax is still soft. Lift
off the pile of newspapers. If you want a 'cracked' effect, like
the veins in a leaf, scrunch up your fabric and attached paper
before soaking it in the dye. Some newspaper may stick to the
fabric but this will come off later.

Batik snowflakes

Part 3 Dyeing the cloth

1   Wearing rubber gloves, immerse your prepared cloth (and any newspaper) in the vat of dye and leave until the required shade is obtained. Remember it always looks much darker at this stage than the final colour.

2   Remove from vat and carefully rinse the fabric in cold water; then pick off as much wax as possible before soaking in hot water to remove more wax and any newspaper.

3   Remove remaining wax by ironing between newspapers. The fabric can then be washed in detergent to soften it and remove any final traces of wax.

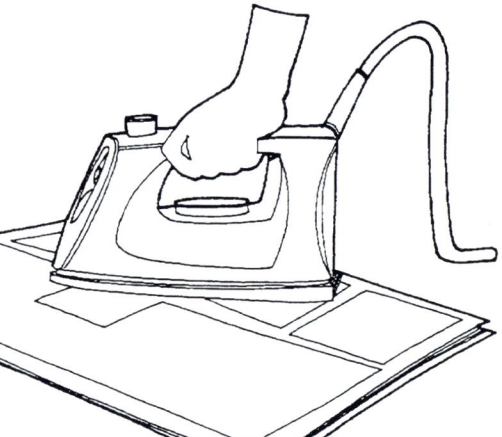

Part 4 Hemming the fabric and evaluating

1   Trim the sides of your fabric to make it square. Roll and pin a narrow hem, taking care to trim and mitre the corners so that they are not too bulky. Tack, removing the pins, and finish with a small machine stitch and press.

2   Compare your fabric with others in your group. You can do this most easily by arranging a large display. Although everyone began with a similar design brief, the patterns will have different features, depending on the design of the patterns and the skills of each worker.

Further/homework

You used axes of symmetry to create a regular pattern. This sort of geometry is used as the basis of patterns from many cultures. Find examples of such patterns, make copies and discuss them with your mathematics teacher.

Fabric constructed by layering is easily damaged by wear, tear and regular cleaning so it is used for decorative purposes only. In this task you will make a layered piece that can be displayed in a deep-sided box frame with no back or front. The fabric will be suspended within it. Light should be able to shine through it.

Part 1: Decorating the fabrics

1   Select a range of different fabrics for layering. If possible choose different fibre types as they will take up the same dye in different ways. Here are some possibilities: cotton muslin, silk chiffon, fine linen, cotton nets, cotton bandage.

2   Decorate each of your chosen fabrics in a different way:

   • batik: you can use random brush stroking of the wax, redipping in the same dye and painting ready mixed dyes onto the scrunched fabric;
   • tie-and-dye: double dyeing with different tying arrangements is effective;
   • spray: using metallic car sprays gives unusual results;
   • fabric paint: although simple, can give bold effects.

Your teacher will help you organize this on a class basis.

3   Now that you have a range of interesting fabrics make some rough sketches of the sort of result you can achieve with them. Use these sketches as a guide for construction.

 Learning

To construct fabric by layering.

 Student's Book

Technical knowledge for textile technology – Layering, page 185 Surface decoration techniques, pages 149–159

 Timing

120 minutes (or less if hand sewing as homework)

 Equipment and materials

• softwood frame (200 mm x 200 mm) made from softwood strips (200 mm x 50 mm x 5 mm)
access to
• vice, hand drill and 2 mm twist drill
• fine wire
• 5 mm dowel rod
• pliers
access to a variety of fabric pieces e.g.
• cotton muslin, silk chiffon, fine linen, cotton nets, cotton bandage
access to a variety of
• threads, feathers, sequins
access to fabric decoration equipment for
• batik, tie-dyeing, fabric painting, spray painting
access to
• iron and ironing board
• needles, sewing machine
• embroidery scissors

 Type of task

Extension

Part 2: Constructing the fabric

1   Use a backing cloth which is fairly transparent but firm and which will not twist. Cut your backing cloth to about 20 cm square.

2   Build up layers of cut or torn shapes from your dyed or other fabrics. You can lay flat objects, feathers, sequins, ribbons, yarns and fibres and so forth between the layers to good effect.

You can pad out areas with toy-stuffing fibres. You can also cut back layers to reveal underlayers or to make holes right through the piece.

3   As you work, tack or stitch the layers in place. This can be done by machine, or by hand – by stabbing through the backing cloth – rather like quilting. Do not worry too much about raw edges as they can enhance the design.

You can add hand-embroidery stitches and areas of intensive free-embroidery machine-stitching.

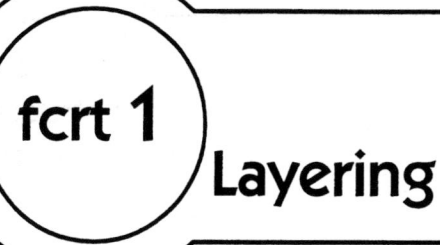

fcrt 1
Layering

fabric
construction
resource
task 1

Part 3: Mounting your fabric

1   When you have finished your piece, make a very narrow hem all round the edge of the backing fabric, rolling the fabric over a strand of fine wire in the top and bottom hems. Make sure that the finished size of your piece is 180 mm square or less. Leave about 10 cm of wire free at all four corners.

2   Construct your box frame. Drill a fine hole near each top corner. Push the ends of the wires through the holes. Pull taut by wrapping the wire ends around small, sanded pieces of fine dowel rod.

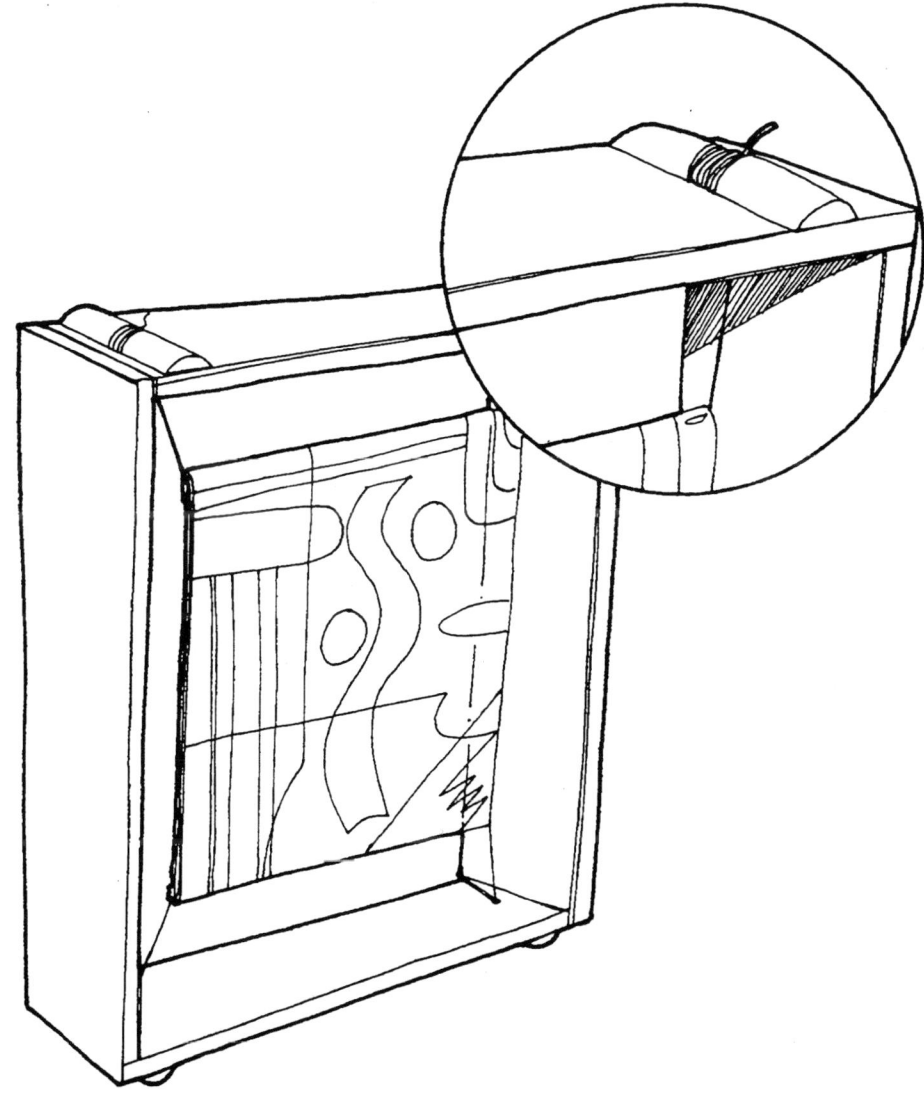

Further/homework

In your workbook, make observational sketches of your finished piece from the front, back and at an angle. Use colour where appropriate.

You will produce a set of small individually-covered buttons that can be used to update an existing garment (cardigan, dress, jacket, waistcoat) or made specifically for a new garment you are designing.

Part 1 Designing the buttons

The buttons will be covered with a closely knitted fabric that you will produce in Part 2. The illustrations show some possibilities:

all one colour and an even texture

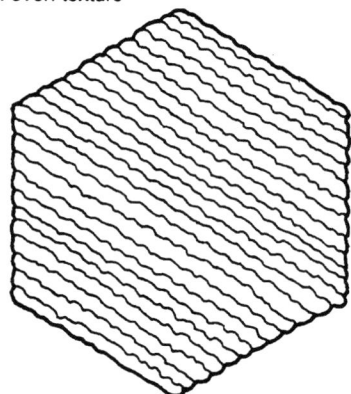

different colours and an even texture

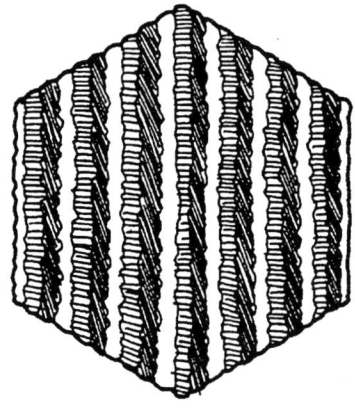

different colours and different textures

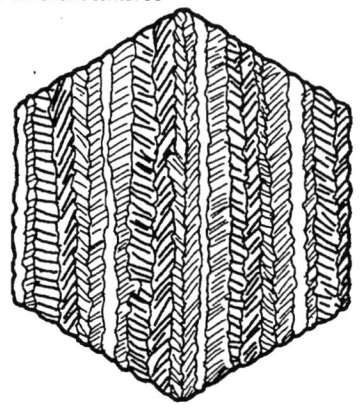

 Learning

To produce fabric by knitting and use the fabric for covering buttons.

 Student's Book

Knitting, pages 182–184

 Timing

120 minutes

 Equipment and materials

- 1 set large buttons (backs and shanks) suitable for covering 30 mm diameter minimum
- assorted crochet yarns and fine knitting threads
- 1 pair very small knitting needles (size 2.75 mm or less)
- scissors
- sewing needles and strong thread.

 Type of task

New

 Other subjects

Mathematics

You can govern the texture by the sort of stitch you use and the sort of thread you choose. You can govern the colour by the thread you choose.

Note down your design decisions by means of annotated sketches. Make sure you label the following:

- the type of thread;
- the colour of thread;
- and the sort of stitches you will use.

Part 2 Knitting hexagons

Now you have to knit a hexagon that will stretch over your size of button.

1   Start with a small number of stitches and then increase the number at each end of the row with each row that you knit, until you have three times as many stitches.

2   When you have completed half your hexagon start reducing the number of stitches at each end of the row. When you get back to your original number of stitches, cast off.

Remember you cannot cut hand-knitted fabric so you may need to experiment in order to get the size right.

You will need to take care when you change from one yarn to another. Ask your teacher for advice.

3   Once you have the size right, knit as many hexagons as you have buttons.

Part 3 Covering the buttons

The illustration shows an exploded view of the button.

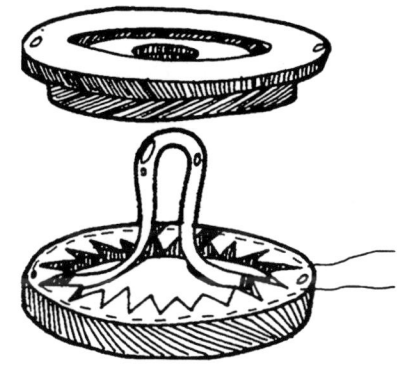

1   Simply place a row of very small running stitches around and close to the edge of the fabric, leaving quite a long loose thread at the beginning and end.

2   Place the head of the button inside the hexagon and, using the loose threads, draw up the excess fabric until it is tight across the shank.

3   Carefully place the base over the shank and press hard into place with finger and thumbs. As it is pushed into place you will hear a dull 'click'. You can then draw out your loose sewing thread and one button is finished. Work in exactly the same way for all the other buttons.

Further/homework

Develop some designs for other items that might use the 'covered with knitting' approach. Here are some suggestions: badges, buckles, brooches, bangles, head bands.

fcrt 3 Investigating the structure of fabrics

In this task you will look at different fabric constructions and investigate the effect this has on the stretchiness of the fabric.

Learning

To understand how the structure of a fabric affects its properties.

Student's Book

Fabrics, pages 178–179

Timing

60 minutes

Equipment and materials

- workbook
- pencil
samples of the following fabric
- different weaves of woollen fabric
- different knits of woollen fabric
- woollen felts of different thicknesses
access to
- hand-lenses
- microscopes
- photocopier for sharing sketches

Type of task

Extension

1 Look at the samples of each fabric as closely as possible using a hand-lens or preferably a microscope.

2 Sketch the arrangement of the fibres.

3 Try to stretch each fabric along its length, width and diagonally. For each stretch sketch the arrangement of fibres.

4 Use your observations to answer these questions.

- How is each fabric constructed?
- What effect does the construction have on the way it stretches?

You may find it useful to work in a group and share your observations and sketches (by using a photocopier).

You may find it useful to record your observations in a table like this:

Fabric type	Arrangement of fibres at rest	Arrangement of fibres when stretched along the length	Arrangement of fibres when stretched along the width	Arrangement of fibres when stretched along the diagonal

Further/homework

1 Look closely at a sample of J-cloth. Sketch the arrangement of fibres.

2 Try to stretch the J-cloth along its width, length and diagonally. For each of these stretches sketch the arrangement of the fibres.

3 Use your observations to answer these questions.

- How is J-cloth fabric constructed?
- What effect does the construction have on the way it stretches?

Fashion accessories: Weaving a small bag

In this task you will produce a piece of woven fabric and use it to make a small bag.

Part 1 Making the fabric

1   Select the ribbons and braids for your fabric. Here are some ways you might make your choice:

- different shades of the same colour;
- two contrasting colours;
- a range of different colours;
- a completely random selection chosen by giving each of six different colours a number from one to six and using a dice.

Note that you can use ribbons and braids of different widths.

 2   Decide on the weaving pattern you want to use.

3   Staple the four corners of the Vilene (shiny side up) to the card. The card will act as your loom.

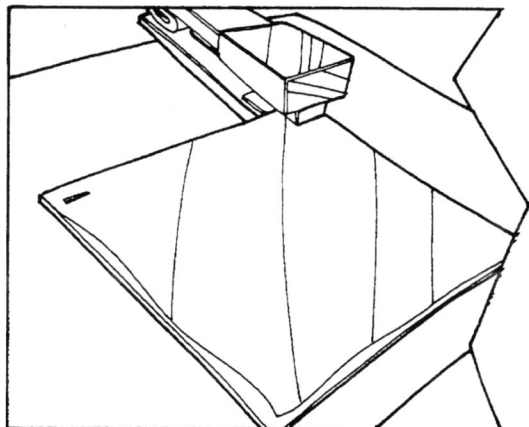

4   Attach the warp ribbons to the Vilene. Pin first along the top so that they are edge to edge with no gaps. Then pin the bottom edge again with no gaps. When you are satisfied with the order hand sew the top and bottom edges to the Vilene.

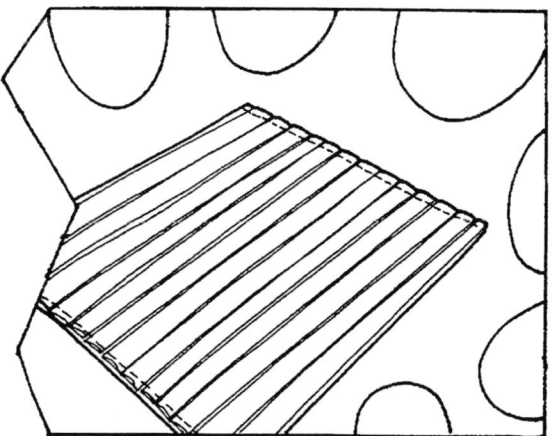

 Learning

To use weaving to construct a fabric.

 Student's Book

Bags and carriers, pages 114–117
Fashion accessories, pages 145–147
Constructing your own fabrics, pages 180–185

 Timing

120 minutes

 Equipment and materials

- 1 piece stiff card (250 mm x 400 mm approximately)
- 1 piece heavy-duty iron-on Vilene (250 mm x 400 mm approximately)
- assorted ribbons and braids, new and recycled length (250 mm and 400 mm)
- stapler
- sewing thread and needles
- scissors
- pins
- 200 mm zip
- lining fabric
access to
- sewing machine
- iron, ironing board and pressing cloth

 Type of task

New

 Other subjects

Mathematics

lirt 1

Fashion accessories: Weaving a small bag

line of
interest
resource
task 1

5   Now weave the weft ribbons into the warp threads in your chosen weaving pattern. Remember:

- attach each ribbon with a pin at the start and at the end;
- ensure that there are no gaps and that the ribbons lie edge to edge;
- if you do not like the effect you are creating simply swap ribbons until you get the effect you like.

6   When you are satisfied with the weaving, hand sew the left and right edges to the Vilene.

7   Now remove the woven fabric and the Vilene backing from the card.

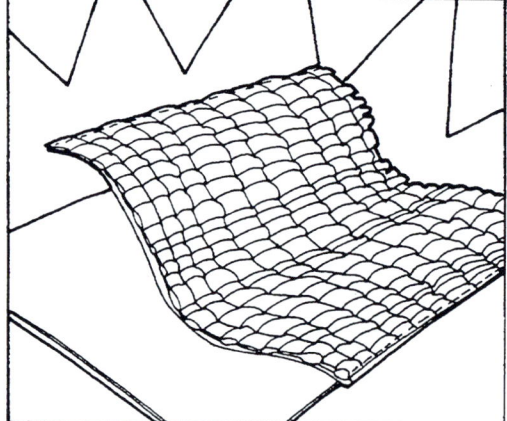

8   Using a damp pressing cloth and iron press the ribbon weave onto the Vilene.

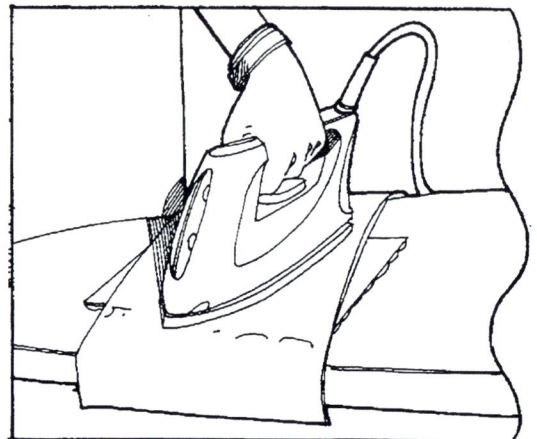

Part 2 Making the small bag

1 Fold your fabric in half and mark out the middle line. Pin across then tack along this line and then remove the pins.

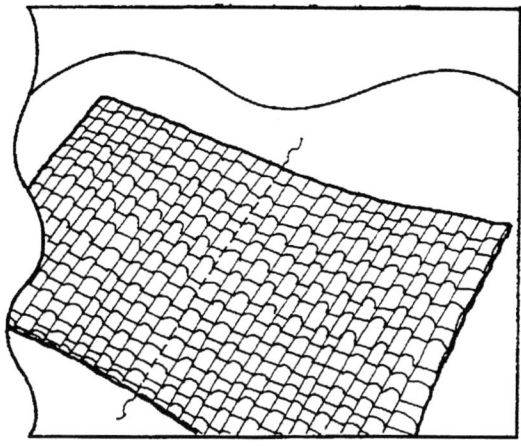

2 Using a sewing machine, sew a line of stitches about 10 mm away on each side of the tacking.

3 Cut along the line of tacking so that you now have two equal-sized and secured pieces of fabric.

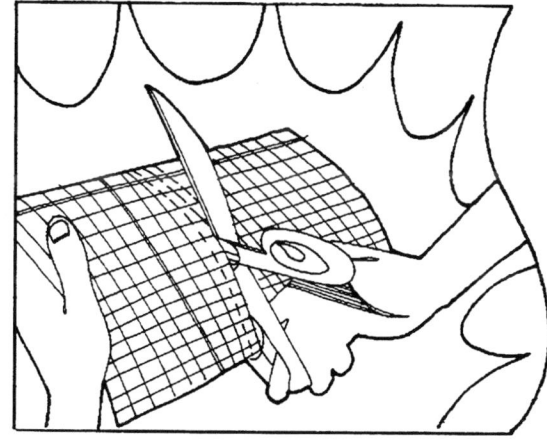

4 Neaten all four sides of each piece using zigzag stitch.

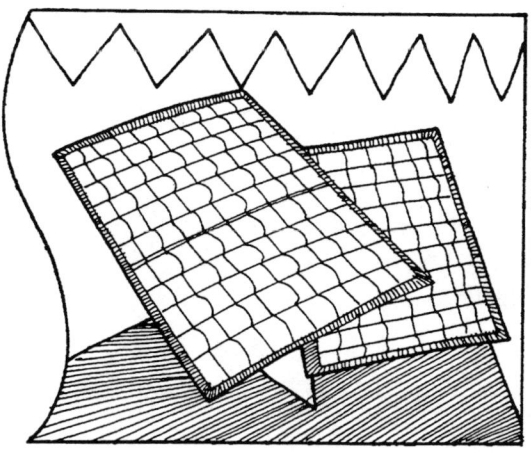

5   Put the right sides together and join the two long sides, leaving a 20 cm gap as shown in the illustration.

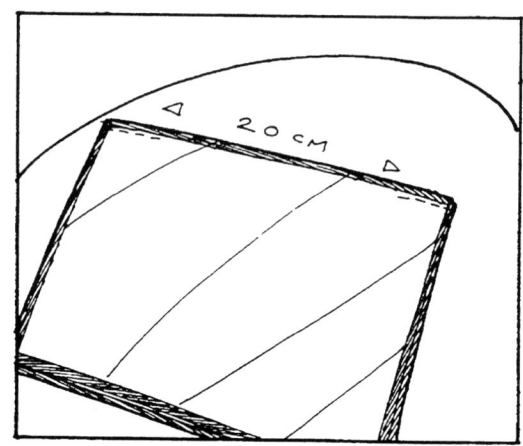

6   Insert the zip into this gap – ask your teacher for help if you are not sure how to do this.

7   When the zip is inserted open it fully, put the right sides together again and tack the remaining edges together.

8   Machine stitch the edges together and trim the corners as shown in the illustration to prevent bulk.

9   Turn the bag inside so that the ribbon fabric is on the outside. Manipulate the seams so that they lie flat and the zip and the corners are well turned out.

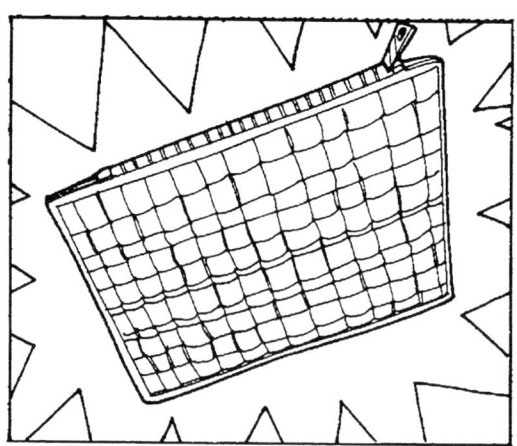

10   Make a lining slightly smaller than the actual bag; insert it into the bag and attach it to the fabric of the zip using slip stitches.

Further/homework

Develop designs for different accessories that might be suitable for ribbon weave fabric.

Bags and carriers: Simple bag decorated with block printing

In this task you will design a simple printing block and use it to decorate a cotton fabric bag.

Part 1: Making the bag

1   Use the outline drawing below to produce the pattern required to make a fabric bag. Cut out the shape required but do *not* assemble until after printing.

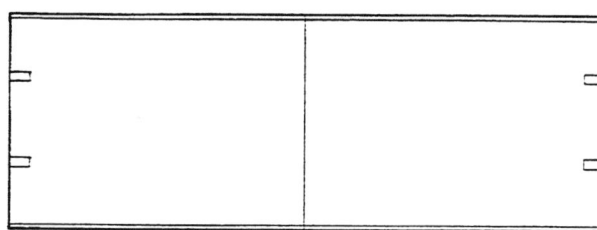

Choose suitable sizes, but make sure that the bag can be made from a single piece of the available fabric

2   Work out your own idea for a handle, and how to attach it to the bag.

Designing the overall appearance of the bag

There are many ways you can use a printing block to decorate the bag. Some are shown in the illustration.

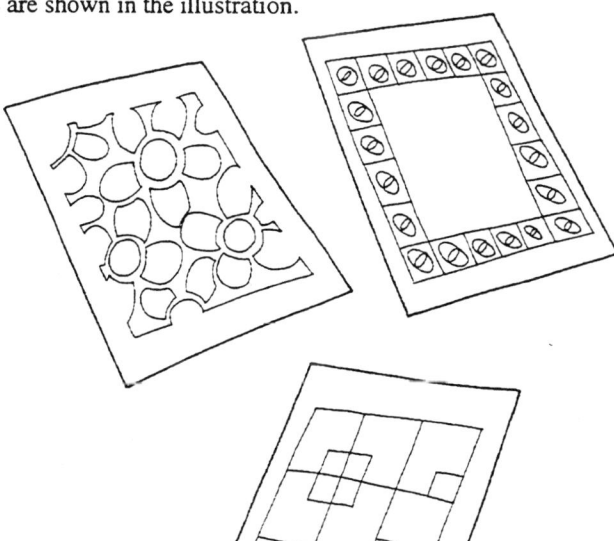

The size of block will vary according to the overall appearance

You will need to decide on the overall appearance of the bag before you choose the size of your printing block.

L **Learning**

To construct a simple fabric bag and decorate it with block printing.

 Student's Book

Bags and carriers, pages 114–117
Block printing, page 155

 Timing

240 minutes

 Equipment and materials

- thin card,
- craft knife
- cutting mat
- printing ink
- tray and roller
- double-sided adhesive tape
- lino

access to

- pattern paper and cotton fabric
- sewing machine
- computer-controlled engraving machine
- wooden bases and handles

t **Type of task**

New

 Other subjects

IT

SAFETY NOTE

Take extreme care when using the craft knife. Hold the material so that your hand is behind the direction of cutting.

Part 2: Producing the printing block the traditional way

1   Produce a simple line 2D image that has meaning for you and could be used as a printing block.

2   Produce a cut-out card version of this image.

3   Try printing the image as shown in the illustration.

4   Modify the card cut-out until you get an image that really pleases you.

5   Use double-sided adhesive tape to attach the card onto a plywood base with a handle so that you can use it easily for block printing.

6   Use the printing block to decorate the fabric of your bag.

7   When the ink is dry sew up the bag and attach the handles.

Part 3: Producing the printing block the IT way

1   Transfer the image onto a computer hard disc either by scanning in from your original design or by drawing from scratch on the screen.

2   Use the image stored in the computer and a computer-controlled engraving machine to cut the image into lino.

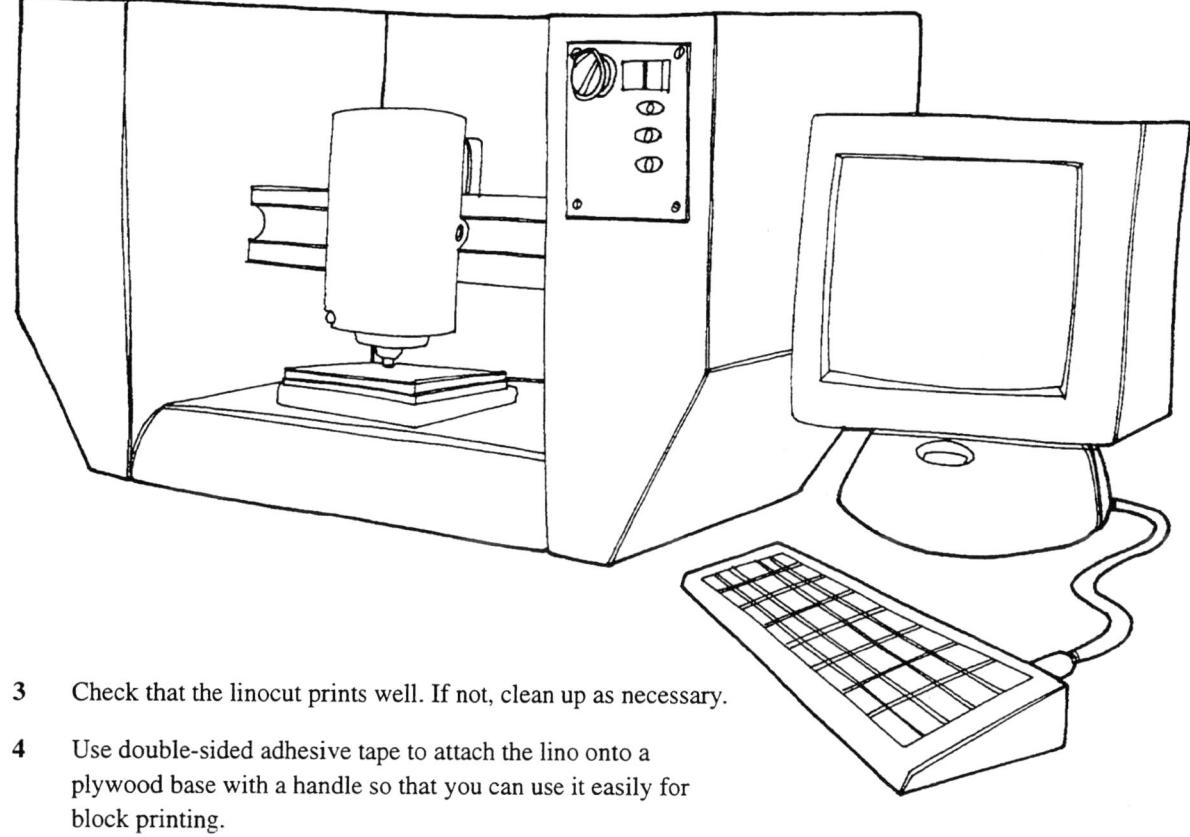

3   Check that the linocut prints well. If not, clean up as necessary.

4   Use double-sided adhesive tape to attach the lino onto a plywood base with a handle so that you can use it easily for block printing.

5   Use the printing block to decorate the fabric of your bag.

6   When the ink is dry, sew up the bag and attach the handles.

Further/homework

You can compare your printing block with the others in the class by producing a poster made up of 20 different prints!

Interiors: Wall hanging for a child's bedroom

In this task you will work in a group of four. Each member of the group will make a felt-embroidered panel to be used in a larger appliqué panel for a child's bedroom.

1   In your group you will need to decide on the following:

- the overall size and shape – square, rectangular, circular, diamond?
- the number of smaller panels needed;
- the design of the smaller panels – animals, plants, everyday objects?
- who will be making each of the smaller panels;
- quality assurance procedures for each part of the wall hanging.

2   Record your decisions, clearly making sure that everyone is in agreement and knows what they have to do and the deadlines for completion.

3   Use the instructions in the Student's book to produce the felt you need in the required colours (page 181). Spend at least five minutes rolling out your sandwich. It's tedious but worth the effort. Leave it to dry and while it is drying, follow numbers **4** and **5**.

4   Carefully draw out a pattern for your motif and cut it out.

SAFETY NOTE
Take care with an electric kettle filled with hot water.

 Learning

To make felt, decorate it with embroidery stitches and use it for appliqué.

 Student's Book

Interiors, pages 118–121
Feltmaking, page 181
Appliqué, pages 157
Embroidery, page 159

 Timing

180 minutes

 Equipment and materials

For feltmaking
- access to wool fibres of different colours
- 2 pieces of calico (200 mm x 200 mm)
- comb
- electric kettle
- washing-up bowl
- rolling-pin

For design
- A3 paper
- coloured pencils

For construction and decoration
- access to strong backing fabric
- access to stiff cardboard
- Copydex adhesive
- assorted embroidery threads, beads and sequins
- wadding
- needles
- scissors
- iron, ironing board and pressing cloth

 Type of task

New

5 Use it as a template to produce three or four outlines on a sheet of A3 paper. Use coloured pencils to explore how you could use embroidery stitches, and the addition of beads and sequins to give your motif detail and texture. The illustration shows some examples of stitches to use.

chain stitch, stem stitch, couching stitch
– all good for line details

herringbone, cross stitch – good for texture infills

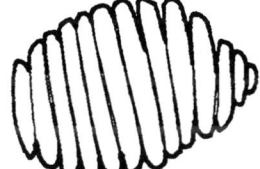

satin stitch
– for a smooth glossy appearance

French knots – singly for eyes and in clusters for flower centres

6 Using a hot iron and a damp pressing cloth press your piece of felt very firmly. This will flatten it further. Take care not to get it wet again.

7 Remove the calico backing and use your pattern as a template for cutting out your motif. Now add the embroidery and other decoration.

8 Now carefully sew your decorated motifs onto your backing fabric. It is important to do this carefully with small stitches. You can place wadding behind the motifs to give a slightly raised effect. To give a stiffness to the wall hanging you can stick the backing fabric to stiff card using Copydex adhesive.

Kites and screen printing

You will produce a simple kite that is easily recognized as your own since it will have a bold screen printed design that can be seen when the kite is flying.

1   Use the information in the Design guide pages 127–131 to produce all the parts you will need to make a hexagon kite. Do not assemble it yet!

2   Design a simple image suitable for screen printing that makes a statement about you. It could be your name, nickname, a cartoon drawing or caricature, or just a lined pattern you find attractive. The illustration shows some examples.

SAFETY NOTE
Take extreme care when using the craft knife. Hold the material so that your hand is behind the direction of cutting.

 Learning

To use basic screen printing techniques to transfer designs onto the kite.

 Student's Book

Screen printing, page 156
Kites, pages 127–131

 Timing

120 minutes (plus homework preparation for design research)

 Equipment and materials

For making a hexagon kite
• kite paper
• dowel
• balsawood for hub
• string

For screen printing
• craft knife, cutting mat, safety ruler
• screen printing frame, ink and squeegee
• materials for making the stencil

 Type of task

New

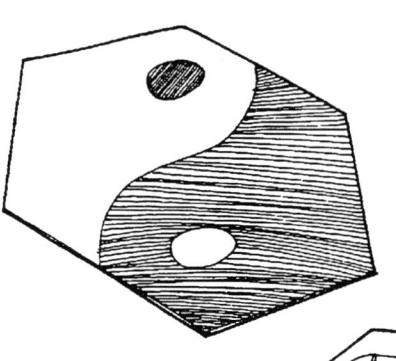

3   Produce the stencil for this image that is the right size for your hexagon kite.

4   Screen print your image onto the kite paper and leave it to dry.

You may wish to experiment with more than one image or with overlapping images.

lirt 4

Kites and screen printing

line of
interest
resource
task 4

5   When the ink has dried assemble your kite.

6   The kites from a class will make an attractive display if they are hung against a wall or from a ceiling. When you look at the display compare the different images and decide which one you think looks the best.

7   You will need to attach a bridle to your kite and a flying line. Then you can fly the kite as a single kite or you can try and produce a train of hexagons as shown below in the illustration.

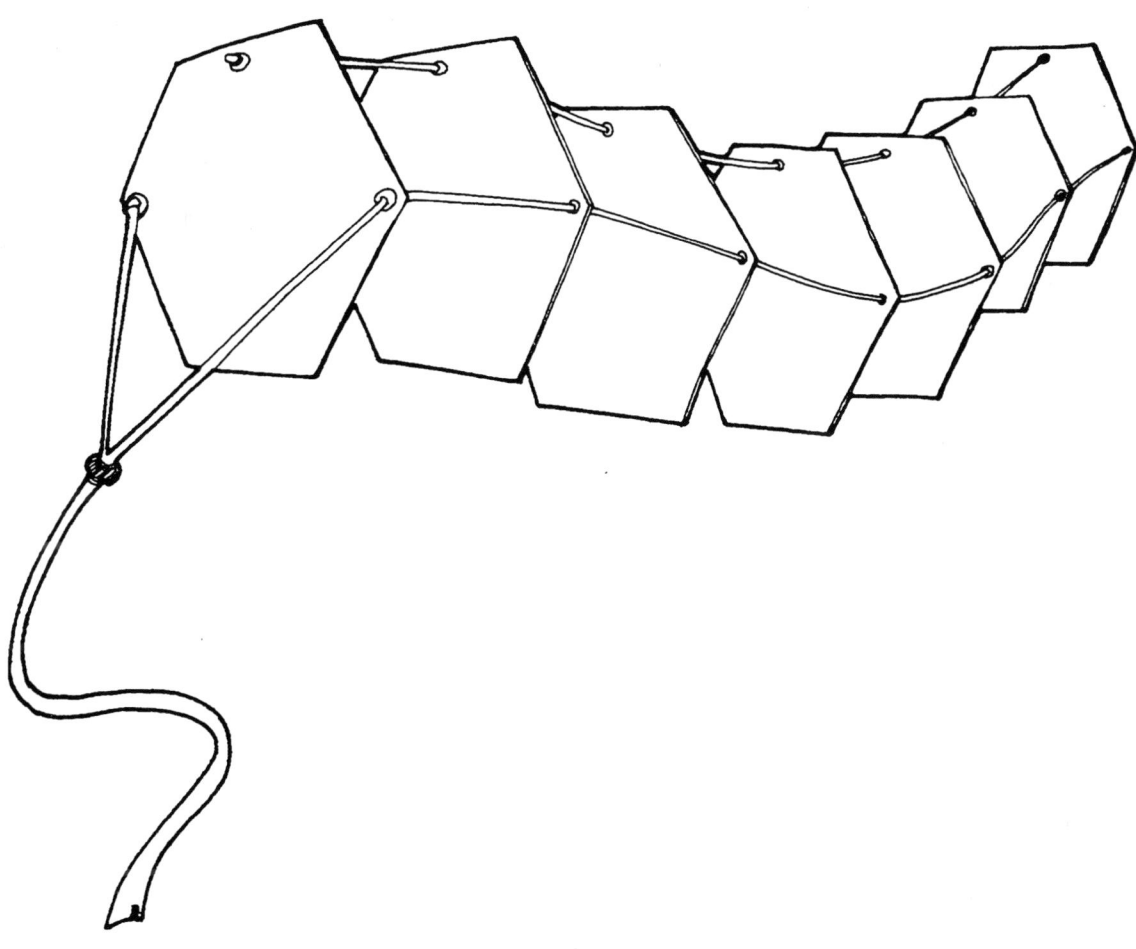

Protection:
Quilted roller-blading mitts

Roller-blading is very popular. Injuries from falling over are seldom all that serious but they are usually quite painful. In this task you will produce a pair of quilted mitts to be worn by a roller-blader as palm protectors.

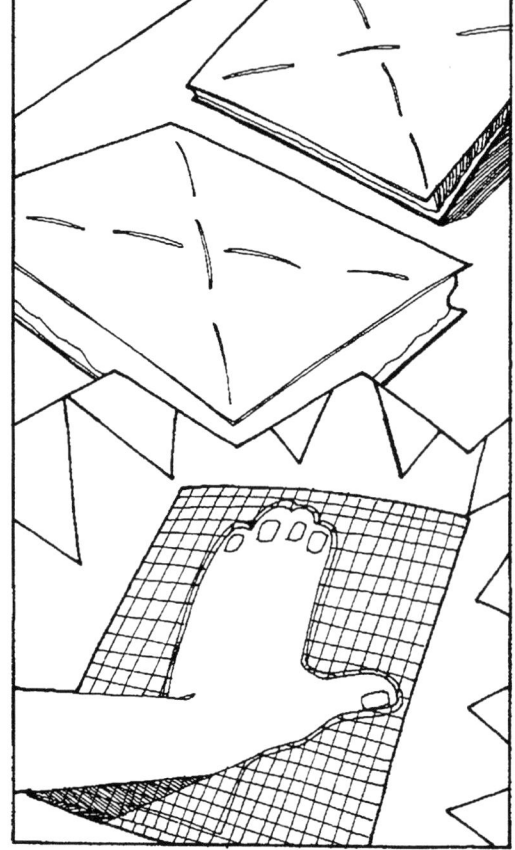

 Learning

To produce a padded fabric by quilting.

 Student's Book

Protection, pages 140–144
Quilting, page 158

 Timing

120 minutes

 Equipment and materials

- squared pattern paper
- 0.5 m closely woven nylon
- 1.25 m of matching or contrasting bias binding (25 mm wide)
- 0.25 m heavy-duty quilting wadding (680 mm wide)
- 0.25 m approximately Velcro
- scissors
- needle and strong thread
- pins
- access to sewing machine

 Type of task

New

Part 1 Making your fabric

1   Cut the nylon into four equal-sized pieces approximately 250 mm x 450 mm. Cut the quilting wadding into two equal-sized pieces 340 mm x 250 mm. Sandwich each piece of wadding between two pieces of nylon.

Protection:
Quilted roller-blading mitts

2   Pin the four corners and across the diagonals of
     each sandwich. Decide on the quilting pattern
     you wish to use. The illustration shows some
     possibilities.

3   Mark on your design with dots and then tack the
     pattern pulling the outer fabrics close together.
     This will prevent slip when machining.

4   Machine the quilting lines using strong sewing
     cotton. A zigzag stitch is easiest to handle. You
     can hand sew the quilting using very small
     backstitch, but this will take longer.

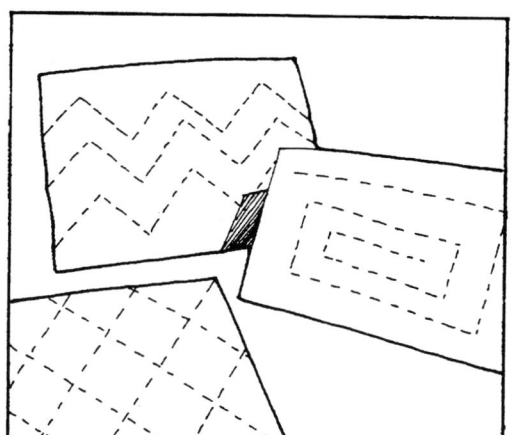

Part 2 Making the pattern

1   Take a sheet of squared pattern paper, fold in half and on each
     side write 'right side up' as shown in the illustration.

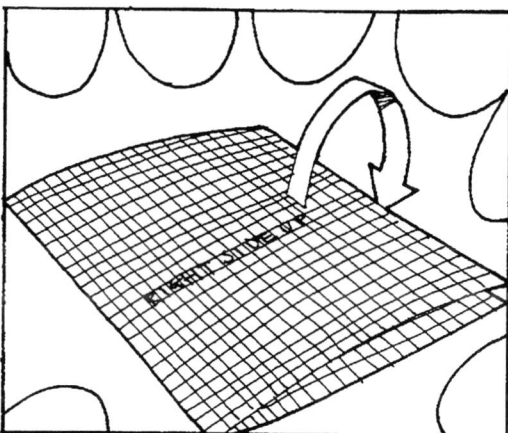

2   Place your hand on the paper with thumb extended and draw
     round your hand, thumb and wrist. Mark lines across where
     your fingers begin and 40 mm down along the wrist. This will
     ensure palm and wrist protection.

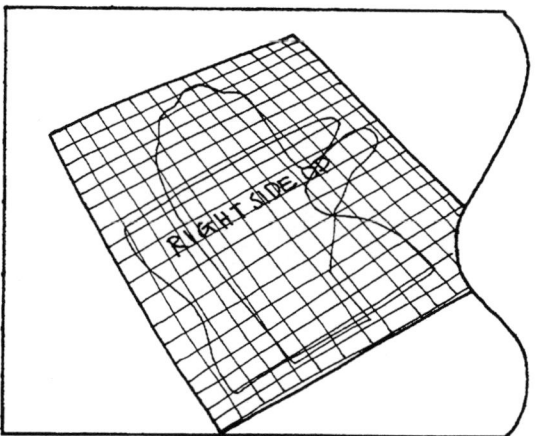

lirt 5

Protection:
Quilted roller-blading mitts

line of
interest
resource
task 5

3 Now add flaps to the outline so that the mitt can do up with Velcro on the back of the hand.

It is better to make the pattern too large at this stage. You can always reduce it but you cannot add on!

4 Cut out your pattern, try it on your hands and make any minor adjustments.

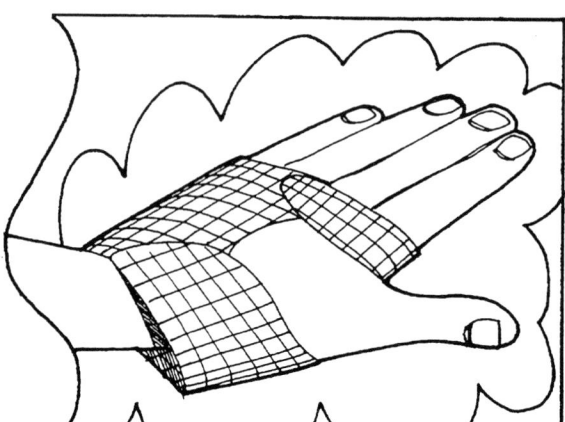

Remember:

- You are not concerned with turning up or hemming; the size you cut is the size you get.
- Ensure there is sufficient wrap-around.
- Ensure there is room to attach the Velcro.
- Make sure there is room for thumb movement.
- If you make any changes make sure both patterns are together and 'right side up' is on the outside of both.

Part 3 Making the mitts

1 Pin each pattern to a sandwich of quilted fabric making sure that each is placed on the correct side of the fabric and 'right side up' is visible.

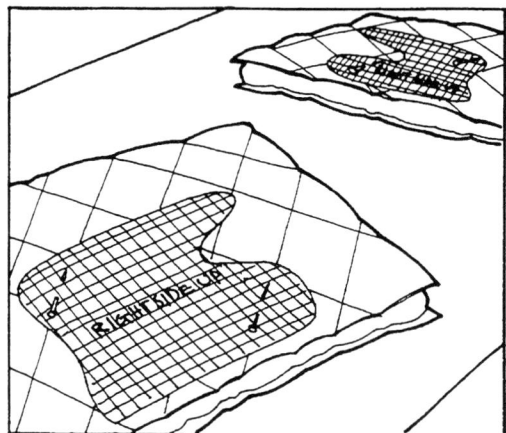

2 Cut out the mitt shapes and, using small tacking stitches, tack all around the edge of each one, 10 mm from the edge.

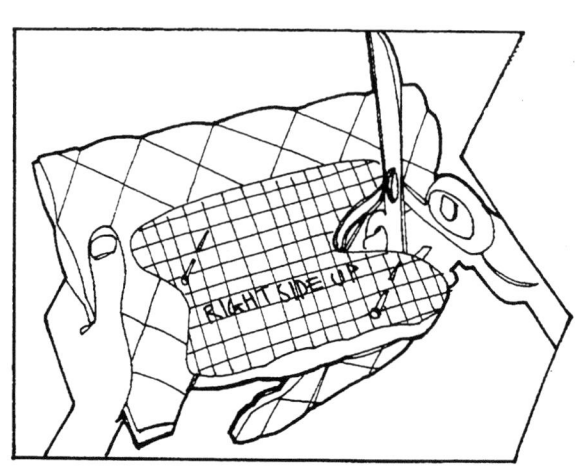

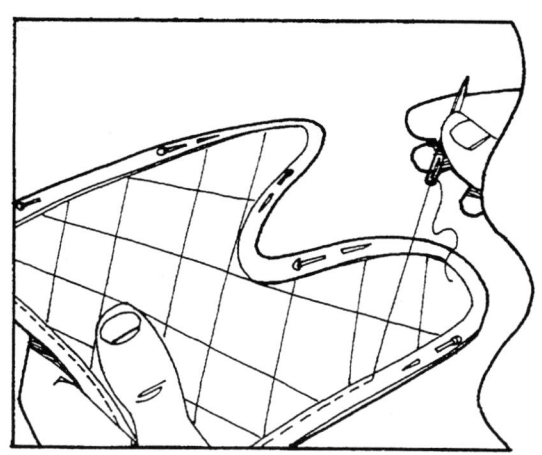

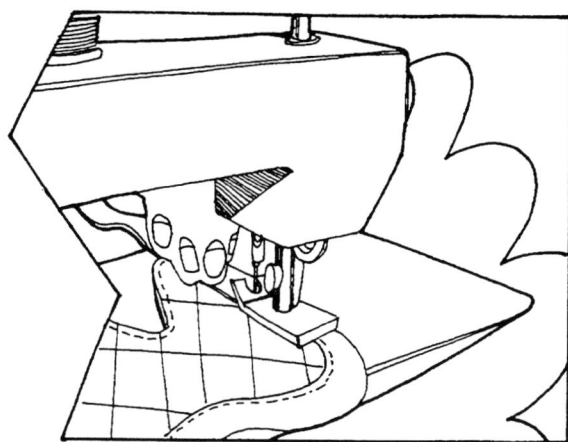

3   On the wrong side of the fabric pin and tack the bias binding in place using the small tacking stitches as a guide. Then machine stitch the bias binding in place.

4   Fold the bias binding over to the other side of the fabric and pin and tack in place. Then finish by hand stitching the binding in place.

Note that because the binding is cut on the bias it will stretch around the shape of the mitts.

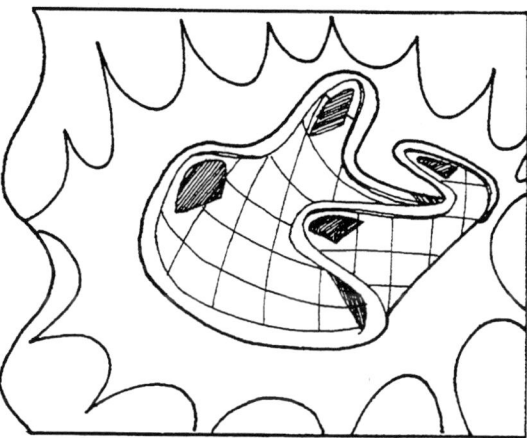

5   Now measure out the Velcro you need to hold the mitts closed. Cut to the required length, pin and machine stitch in place.

Your mitts are finished – happy blading!

Further/homework

Develop designs for a simple protector to be worn by roller-bladers on their elbows and knees.

In this task you will design decorations for a T-shirt or baseball cap and apply them by transfer printing and spray painting. Make sure your item has been washed, dried and pressed.

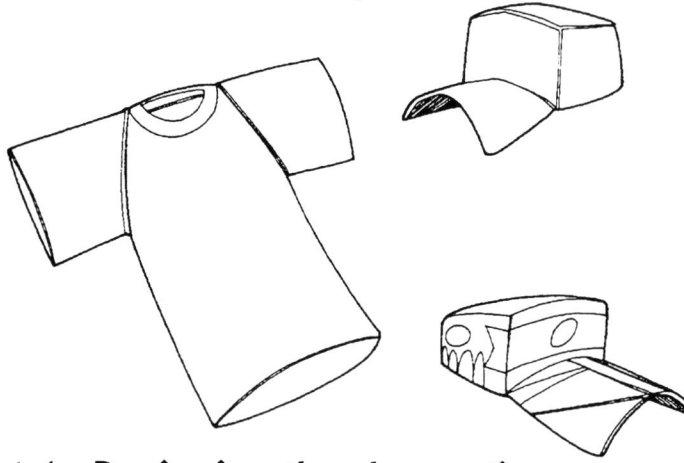

Part 1: Designing the decoration

1   Your design should meet the following criteria:

- it should be original;
- it should be personal;
- it should have street cred.

One way to tackle this is to list your interests in popular culture and make a collage about these using images from popular magazines. You can include pictures about music, films, computer games, fashion, TV and video – anything that you're interested in.

Think about what sort of statement you want to make about yourself. Once you have this collage use a hole template to identify parts that might meet the criteria above.

 Learning

To decorate with transfer printing and spray painting.

 Student's Book

Transfer printing, Spray-Painting, page 153–154
Street style, pages 122–126

 Timing

120 minutes

 Equipment and materials

- iron-on transfer paint or transfer printing inks
- brushes
- spray bottle or spray-diffuser and jar
- old toothbrush and spatula
- thin card
- scalpel and board
- paper
- iron and board
- washed, dried, light-coloured, plain-peak baseball cap or light coloured T-shirt
- work-book
- pencil
- coloured pencils
- access to popular magazines

 Type of task

New

lirt 6

Street style: Transfer printing

line of
interest
resource
task 6

2   In your work-book, use these images to make
    some rough sketches of suitable ideas.

3   Sketch out an area roughly the size and
    shape of the area you want
    to print. Transfer one of
    your ideas to this area.
    Develop this and/or other
    ideas. Remember that with
    transfer printing everything
    prints out as the other way
    round – so you must be
    particularly careful about letters
    and numbers.

Part 2: Preparing the transfer

1   On paper, lightly draw the shape and details of your final print
    design.

    •   Use transfer inks or paints with brushes for the solid colour
        areas.
    •   Use a spray-diffuser, spray bottle or toothbrush (splatter
        paint by running a spatula across the bristles) for the spray
        paint areas.
    •   Use a stencil or card edges to limit the spray spread.

2   Allow your design to dry.

Part 3: Making the print

1   Place the paper design face down on the fabric area to be
    printed. Set the iron to medium. Smooth over the back of the
    paper with the iron for about 20 seconds.

2   Peel off the paper carefully, to reveal your design.

Further/homework

Develop some ideas for another transfer/spray print. This should also
reflect street style. Your design should be at least 30 cm square.

1   Cut or tear the design into three or four sections or strips.
    Collage the pieces back together.

2   Trace off the resulting design. Transfer the tracing to plain
    paper. Then use transfer paints or inks to colour your design, as
    before.

3   Print it onto cloth (to make a simple bag) or a T-shirt.

Tents: Investigating seams, reinforcements and loops

Part 1 How waterproof are seams?

You will investigate five different seam constructions to see which construction is the most waterproof. You will need to construct a sample for each of these seams. In order for your investigation to be a fair test it is important that the only difference between the samples is the type of seam; the fabric, thread, stitch size, stitch type and needle used should be the same for each seam.

1   Use a waterproof cloth, such as ripstop nylon. Decide on the other details and make a note of your decisions.

2   Make your seam samples – just straight seams – joining two pieces of material as shown in the illustration.

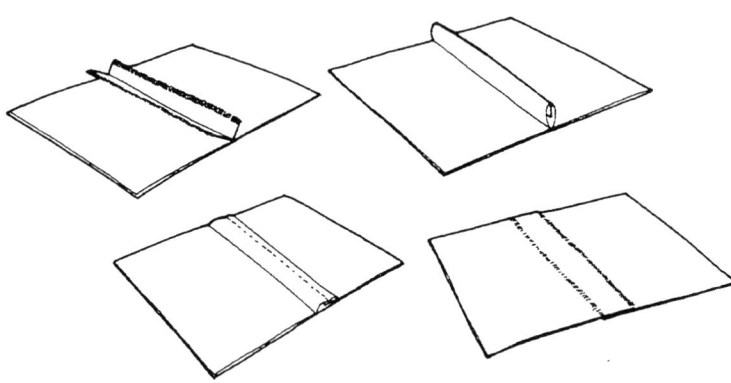

3   Now you have to decide on the best way to test for the 'waterproofness' of each seam. The illustration shows some possibilities. Remember for the test to be fair you will need to test each seam in exactly the same way.

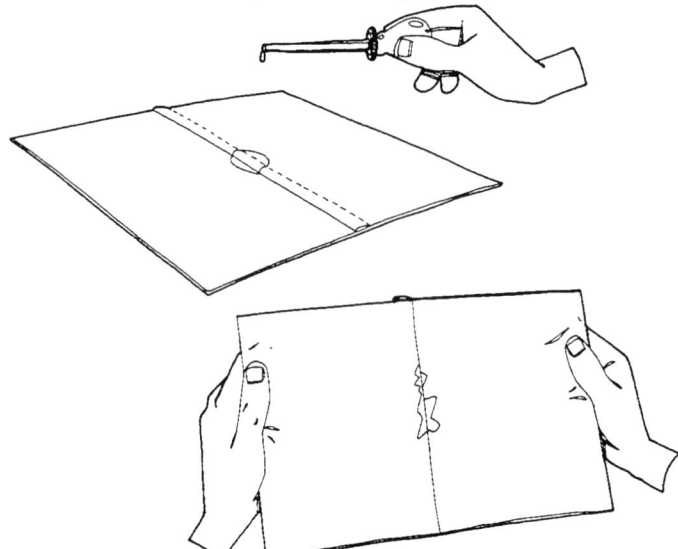

How will you make sure each seam gets the same amount of water?

Learning

- To practise seams, machine sewing, testing and evaluating.
- To make and test reinforcements and loops.

Student's Book

Tents design guides, pages 177–179
Construction techniques for tents and kites, pages 211–212

Timing

Part 1: 1 hour
Part 2: 1 hour

Equipment and materials

Part 1
- 8 pieces (16 cm x 8 cm) of ripstop nylon or other waterproof cloth
- thread
- machine/machine needles
- shears
- water spray
- drop pipette
- beaker
- paper kitchen towel
- drying line

Part 2
- cloth samples
- fusible interlinings
- glues
- workbook
- pencil

Type of task

Recap and extension

Other subjects

Science

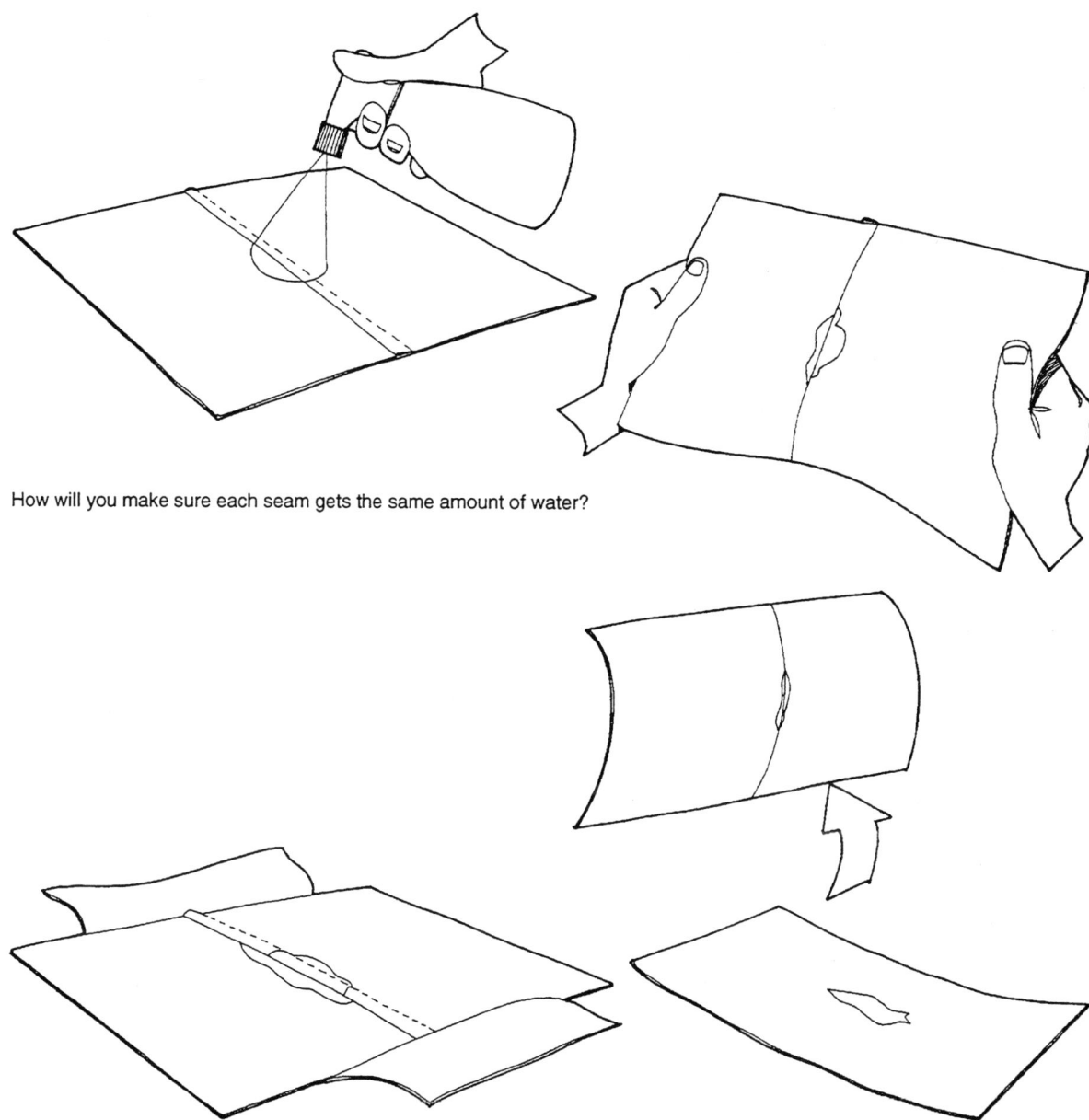

How will you make sure each seam gets the same amount of water?

How will you measure or compare the stain areas?

4   Discuss which methods you will use with other students in your group. By co-operating and sharing data you can get results from several different methods.

5   Describe your investigation using annotated drawings. Record your results in table form.

6   Use your results and those of other groups to put the seams in an order of waterproofness.

7   Try to explain why some seams perform better than others.

Part 2 Investigating reinforcements

Most tents need reinforcing at points of particular stress. The illustrations show some examples.

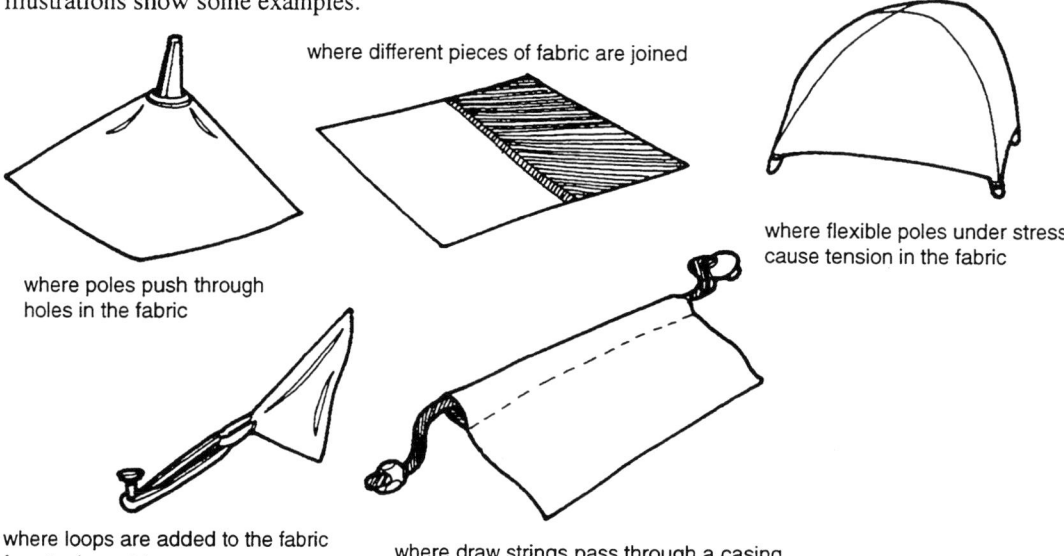

where different pieces of fabric are joined

where poles push through holes in the fabric

where flexible poles under stress cause tension in the fabric

where loops are added to the fabric for attachment to guy-ropes

where draw strings pass through a casing

In all these places there may be a need for reinforcement. The difficulty facing the tent designer is to decide on the *nature* and *extent* of the reinforcement.

- Is it simply a case of more of the same sort of stitches or would it be better to use different stitches or perhaps a different thread?
- Will adding extra fabric to a part under stress help? If so, what sort and thickness of fabric should be used? How should it be held in place?
- Might it be possible to introduce a resistant material into the fabric at the point of stress – a metal ring where a tent pole passes through a hole in the fabric for example?

The illustration shows some possible ways of reinforcing.

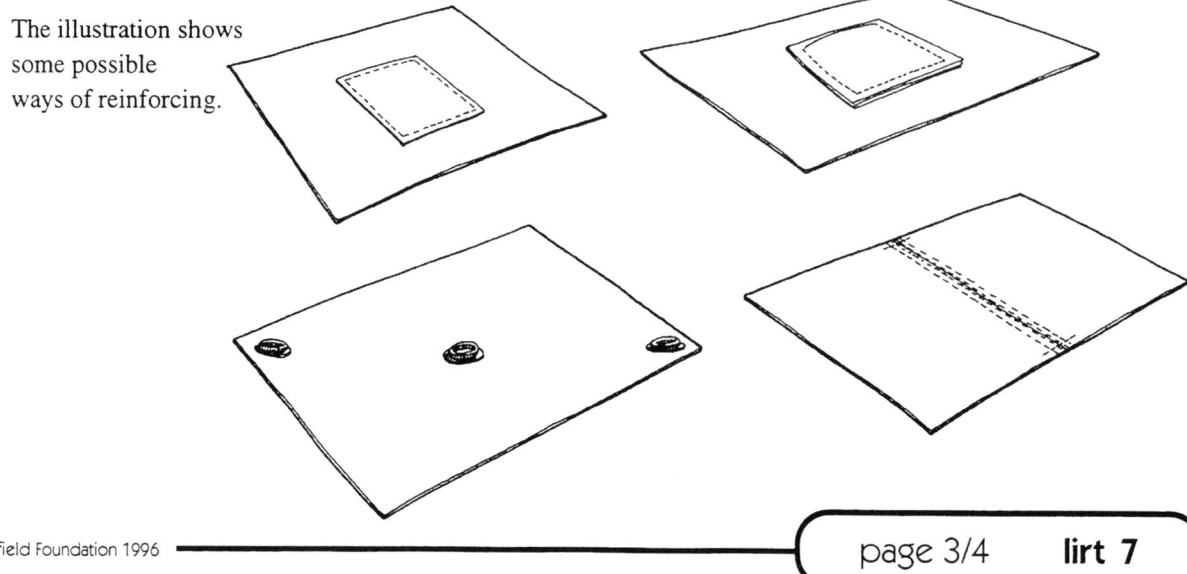

1   Make up four different samples in which you think there is a need for reinforcement. (If you work in a group you can do this more efficiently.)

2   Decide how each sample should be reinforced and make an improved reinforced version.

3   Now devise a simple test to compare the two versions.

4   Describe your investigation using annotated drawings. Record your results in table form.

5   Using your results, describe the effectiveness of your reinforcements.

Further/homework: Investigating loops

Fabric loops are used in the construction of tents. They can fail in a number of ways:

- the fabric can tear causing the loop to 'come open';
- the stitching holding the fabric in a loop can fail causing the loop to 'come open';
- the stitching holding the loop to another piece of fabric can fail causing the loop to become detached.

Design and carry out a series of simple experiments to investigate the performance of loops.

In this task you will make 3D hearts to be worn by six performers in a romantic musical who will dance to the song, 'That feeling called love'. The hearts will be worn over an all-black costume and held on by means of black tape with a quick-release fastening such as Velcro. You will need to work in a team of three with each team member making two hearts.

 Learning

To use darts to achieve 3D textile forms.

 Student's Book

Theatre design guides, pages 132–136
Making your product – joining and shaping, pages 201–212

 Timing

120 minutes

 Equipment and materials

- workbook
- pencil
- paper for patterns
- card
- scissors
- shears
- sewing machine
- thread
- needles
- stuffing materials
- black fabric tape
- Velcro
- red polyester cotton

 Type of task

New

1 Sketch out a heart shape of suitable size.

2 Add tape details.

3 Make a 2D model to check that heart shape cond size and tape lengths are suitable.

4   Make a first draft pattern for the back and the front. Note the following points:

- no need to include seam allowance at this stage;
- front will be larger than back;
- include dart details;
- include matching notches.

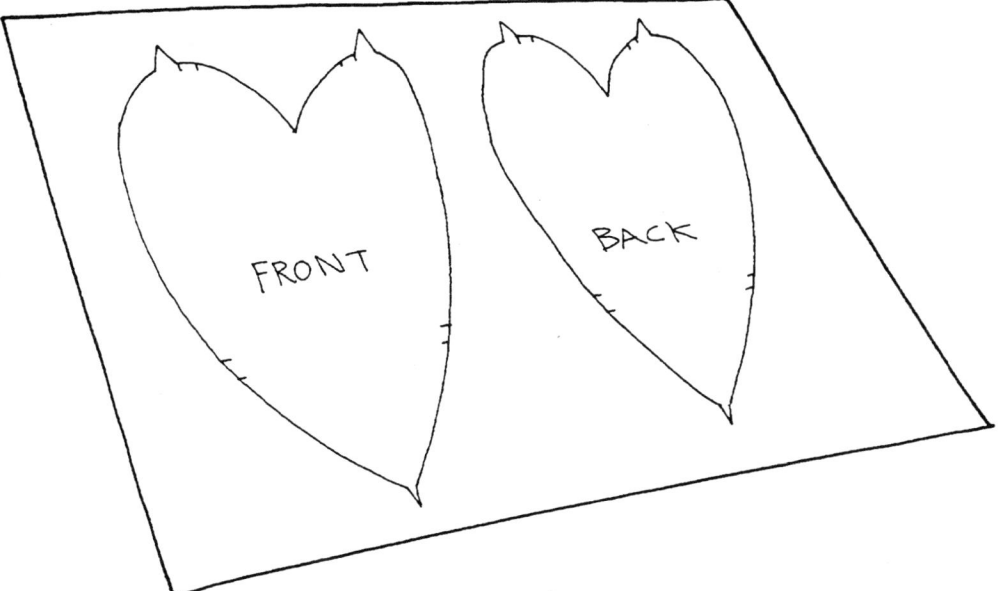

5   Use your first draft pattern to check the following:

- that the darts give you the 3D form that you want; adjust if necessary;
- that the back and front fit together accurately;
- that the notches match.

6   Now make a second draft with any necessary changes. Include a seam allowance and add all necessary details.

7   Using your pattern make up a 3D heart in red polyester. Remember to leave a gap for adding the stuffing.

8   Attach the black tapes and Velcro.

9   Add the stuffing, and once you have a satisfactory 3D form hand sew the closing.

Further/homework: Costumes for the 'Don't you want me?' dance

Develop patterns for a broken heart. The heart should start looking as if it is one piece but as the dance proceeds it should break into two or three pieces. You will need to design ways of keeping the pieces together before the heart breaks, ways of keeping the different pieces apart but still held onto the performer, and ways of rapid putting together for when the dancer finds a new love.

Health and safety

1   In this task you will think about the situation illustrated here. You can do this task on your own or with a partner. You will need to use a table like this:

Hazard	Risk	Risk assessment	Risk control

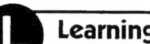 **Learning**

To revise and extend your understanding of how to be safe, and ensure the safety of others.

 Student's Book

Health and safety, pages 213–214

 Timing

40 minutes

 Equipment and materials

- workbook
- pen, pencil
- large sheets of paper and big pens

 Type of task

Recap and Extension

2   Complete your grid by working across the page – hazard, risk, assessment, control. Then go on to the next hazard – and so forth. You should not simply be looking for the likely isolated hazards – you should particularly think about the interactions between the various elements in the illustrated situation.

Further/homework

Find out more about people who work at home, their legal situation, and the organizations that aim to support them.

In this task you will look closely at a pair of shorts. Work in a group and use your observations and discussions to answer these questions. Include annotated drawings in your answers where appropriate.

1   Manufacture:

- What type of fabric has been used?
- How suitable is it?
- What type of seam has been used?
- Do you think it was a good choice?
- What type of fastening has been used?
- Does it allow easy access?
- How are the shorts finished?
- What additional features have been added?
- Are there any improvements you could make?

2   Fitness for purpose:

- What is their intended purpose for wearing?
- How often will they be worn?
- How easy are they to put on and take off?
- How easy are they to wash and iron?
- How well will they fit? How comfortable will they be?

3   Origin:

- What fibres are in the shorts?
- Where have these come from?
- What type of fabric is used?
- Where might this have been made?
- Where were the shorts manufactured?
- Who might have manufactured them?
- Where would you buy shorts like this?
- How much would they cost?
- How much would the maker be paid?
- Why is there likely to be a large difference between the last two answers?

Learning

To extend your understanding of how to investigate products.

Student's Book

Evaluating, pages 96–98
Identifying needs and likes, pages 70–77

Timing

80 minutes

Equipment and materials

- workbook
- pen, pencil
- access to a pair of shorts

Type of task

Revision and Extension

part 1

Investigating a single product

products
and applications
resource
task 1

4   A closer look at manufacturing.

(a) Draw a sketch showing the different parts that make up the shorts – an exploded view like the one shown here would be best.

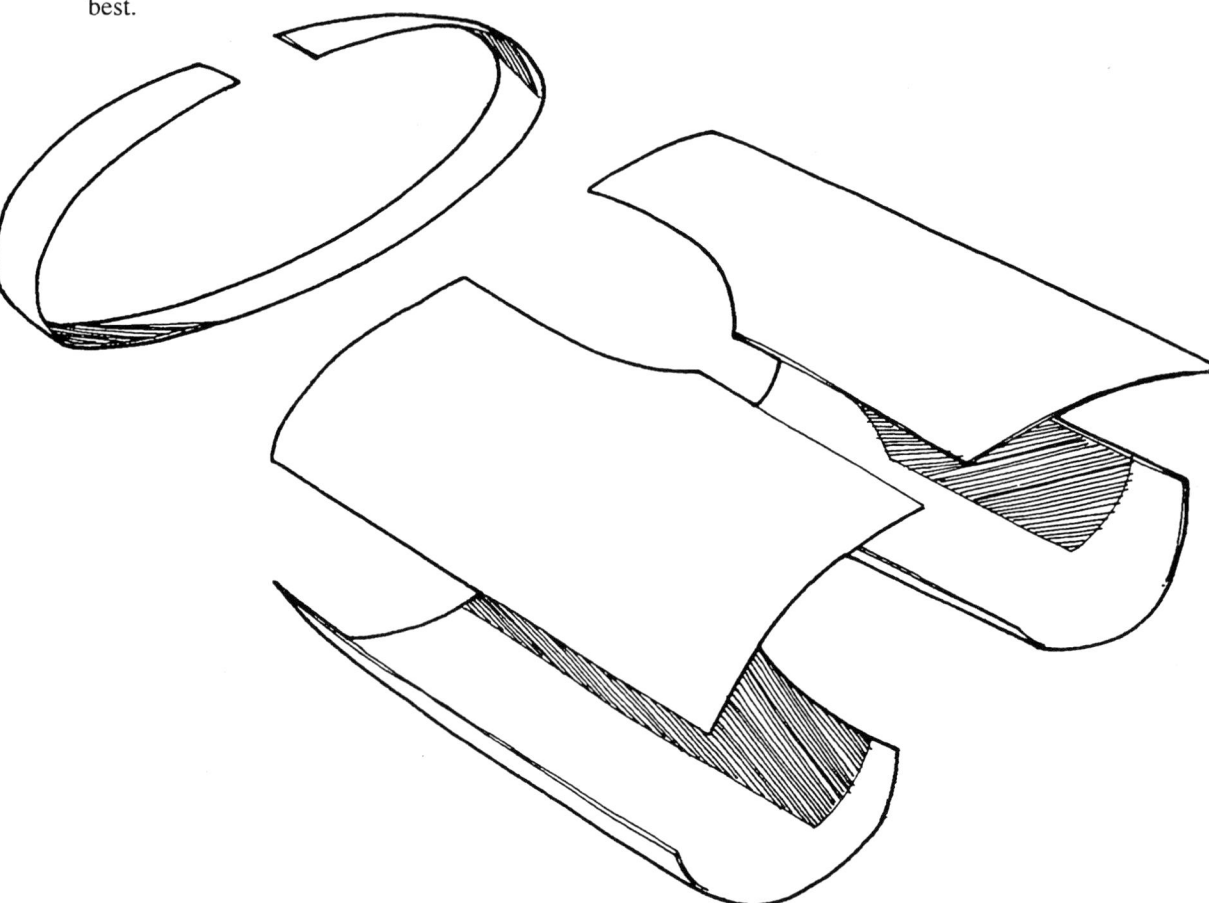

(b) Develop a flow chart that would allow easy manufacture of the garment in a batch of 100 using five workers. You can assume that all the pieces are available ready cut. (Note that this is not quite as simple as it may seem. Some operations take longer than others and can result in 'bottle-necks'.)

(c) Talk through your flow chart with other students to identify any difficulties and adjust your manufacturing flow chart accordingly.

(d) When you have a successful solution check it with your teacher.

Further/homework

So far you have only considered the assembly of the shorts from pre-cut parts. Extend your manufacturing flow chart to show how the shorts are handled so that they arrive packaged for display and sale in the sports departments of a chain of large retail stores.

Shorts have been fashion favourites for a long period of time. There have been many styles and fads, some of which are shown below, but they are all recognizable as shorts despite variations in fabric, decoration and cut. In this task you will look closely at a collection of pairs of shorts.

Learning

To extend your understanding of how to investigate products.

Student's Book

Evaluating, pages 96–98
Identifying needs and likes, pages 70–77

Timing

80 minutes

Equipment and materials

- workbook
- pen, pencil
- access to a collection of shorts

t **Type of task**

Revision and Extension

1   Work in a group and use your observations and discussions to answer the questions in the table on page 2, 'Investigating a collection of textile products'.

Investigating a collection of textile products

Feature	Product 1	Product 2	Product 3	Product 4
Who is likely to buy or wear these?				
Where are they likely to be sold?				
On what occasions are they likely to be worn?				
How much are they likely to cost?				
What fibres are in them?				
What is the type of fabric?				
Where might fibre and fabric come from?				
What types of seam have been used?				
What fastenings have been used?				
Where were they manufactured?				
How much is machine-made and how much hand made?				
Has the fabric been decorated in any way? If so how?				
How might the shorts be advertised/marketed?				
How long are they likely to last, given normal wear?				
How are they to be cared for?				

2   Use the information in your completed table to answer the following questions:

   (a) In what ways are the products similar?

   (b) In what ways are the products different?

   (c) Why are there so many different sorts of shorts available on the market?

   (d) If you had money to set up a business manufacturing shorts, which kind of shorts would you manufacture? Give reasons for your answer.

Further/homework

Use the information in your table to help you develop a design for shorts aimed at the following consumer groups:

- young teenagers;
- health-conscious young adults;
- overweight adults;
- elderly people;
- those concerned with recycling and the environment;
- those concerned with promoting a healthy lifestyle for all.